Oh boy!

Oh boy!

Understanding the neuroscience
behind educating and raising boys

Dr Michael C. Nagel

First published as *Boys Stir Us: Working with the Hidden Nature of Boys* in 2006 and republished as *Educating and Raising Boys* in 2020 by Hawker Brownlow Education.
This revised and updated edition is published by Amba Press in 2021.

Amba Press
Melbourne, Australia
www.ambapress.com.au

Editor – Natasha Harris
Cover designer – Alissa Dinallo
Printed by IngramSpark

ISBN: 9781922607065 (pbk)
ISBN: 9781922607072 (ebk)

A catalogue record for this book is available from the National Library of Australia.

This book is dedicated to my son, Harrison, or Harry as he is known to family and friends. My little boy yesterday, my friend today, my son forever. A fine young man who I could not be prouder of in all that he is and all that he does!

Contents

Illustrations

Figures

Tables

Acknowledgements

For all of my life I have been involved in education in some way, shape or form. During this time I have met many fantastic parents and teachers. I have also met many amazing boys and young men. Unfortunately I have also witnessed a worrying trend. Over the last few decades, and at a time of increased affluence, boys have continued to struggle in school and in many aspects of life. I have studied this as researcher and later with a vested interest as a father and found that boys do need help, mentorship and guidance. And while each boy is unique unto himself, all boys share many similarities in how they engage with the world around them ... a world that often fails to recognise or pay enough attention to a myriad of biological and physiological differences between boys and girls. Moreover, for some people even the notion of discussing the biological differences between boys and girls can set off a firestorm of condemnation wrapped in spurious notions of equality. Boys and girls are different and while some of this is shaped by our cultural and social norms, many differences are also the result of the complex nature of the chemical and structural aspects of the brain. This book explores those differences and draws on my experiences and the experiences of others who have helped shape my views, extend my knowledge and support my endeavours. To them I must say thanks.

First, my boyhood journey was not always smooth but I was blessed to have had four amazing friends help me find my way when needed.

These boyhood friends became lifelong 'brothers' who still influence my sense of self and my continuing journey in different ways as adults. To Bryan, Dan, Enio and Reg, I say thank you for being who you are and for your part in helping me become who I am in your own unique and special ways!

Second, it is important to acknowledge all those parents who do their best to raise fine young men. If only there were one manual for how to raise children life would be easier but it would also be much less interesting and rewarding. There is no magic bullet for raising children, but with patience and love almost anything is possible and most challenges manageable. Always remember, you are the foundation of everything your child needs to manage the ups and downs of life.

Third, to all the teachers who spend countless hours working to enhance the lives of all children, male or female, thank you! Your tireless efforts should never go unnoticed, and this is just my small way of saying you are appreciated and indispensable for so many boys!

Next, it would be remiss of me not to acknowledge the support of my university and thank all those at the University of the Sunshine Coast that I call colleagues and friends. And equally important are the people of Amba Press for refining my work and making it available to the masses. A special thanks to Natasha Harris for bringing greater coherence and clarity to my writing. And most importantly to Alicia Cohen for her openness to ideas, candour in thought, strength in conviction and continued faith in what I do.

And most importantly, to Laura, my best friend and partner in life ... a never-ending supporter of me. Thank you for grounding me and making my life beautiful!

Introduction

A war on boys?

All boys are human, even when there is reason to suspect the contrary. I mean that they are a fair sampling of humanity, with the right proportion of cheats, liars, dolts, heroes, and geniuses. A teacher finds it important to remember this fact.[1]

Boys are, for instance, far more likely to harm themselves or to be involved in accidental death than are girls.[2]

Boys will top the class in accidents and assaults and they will be the bottom of the class in literacy and learning.[3]

... as a group, boys are in trouble. Not every boy, not in the same kind of trouble and not all of the time – but enough of them across all ethnic and socio-economic groups to know there is a pattern.[4]

What is not in dispute is that boys need help.[5]

Despite the fresh attention being paid to the problems of boys, many of the key indicators tracking how boys are faring, are getting worse, not better.[6]

The quotes above do not paint a very pretty historical picture of boyhood. Even Plato himself has been credited with a degree of concern about boys in noting that 'of all the animals, the boy is the most unmanageable.'[7] In the 1940s when Jacques Barzun penned the first quote offered above, he became one of many individuals throughout history lamenting the challenges associated with raising and educating boys. Today there are contemporary reasons to be even more concerned about growing up male – there is no shortage of evidence showing that boys lag behind girls in many measures of achievement and wellbeing. For example, the Organisation for Economic Co-operation and Development (OECD) notes that, worldwide, boys are more likely than girls to fail to attain a baseline level of proficiency in reading, maths and science.[8] Such examples seem to suggest that boys are a problem, or at the least, problematic, which in turn often leads to agendas to 'fix' the problem.

For some, fixing the problem of, or problems with, boys too often focuses on how aspects of masculinity do not align with 'proper' educational and social conduct. Sociologists and sociocultural theorists, for example, argue that challenges and issues associated with boys are founded on the interplay of masculinity, social structures and cultural norms. Critics of such perspectives argue that these views often result in an agenda to 'change' boys that quickly become an actual war on boys and 'boyhood.'[9] While there is certainly plenty of evidence to suggest that there may indeed be some kind of ideological 'war' on boys or boyhood, there are also plenty of apathetic views related to boys. At the other end of the continuum, for example, can be found many who use the catchcry 'boys will be boys' to explain inappropriate behaviour without any consideration of why that behaviour occurred! I would argue that both positions either omit, or fail to recognize, any notion of 'innateness' in what it means to be male and, in particular, how such innate tendencies may be the by-product of the brain and mind. Therefore, perhaps it is timely to look at what a boy might actually be, or, more colloquially, what a boy might be made of. New advances in science and medical research allow us to go beyond the nursery definition of 'snakes and snails and puppy dog tails' and offer a more contemporary perspective. In particular, the field of neuroscience has opened a whole new world of understanding the intricacies of being human and, indeed, being male.

Since the end of the last century we have learned more about the brain than had ever been known prior to this time. Now we can actually witness, in action, the neurophysiology and neurobiology of males and females alike. Continued advances in medical research and neuroscience offer very revealing data suggesting that the brains of boys maintain certain characteristics that may impact on their emotions, approaches to learning, personality and temperament, sense of identity and overall sense of wellbeing. An abundance of research also exists that identifies different neurological intricacies between boys and girls that can be explained by looking at the unique structural and chemical differences found between and within the brain of each sex.[10]

Examining the neuroscientific research about the male brain allows us to develop a new perspective in working with and attending to the needs of boys. Rather than looking to somehow fix the problem of 'boyhood', what we must do is modify our perspective of boyhood and boy behaviour. We need to have a greater understanding of the very biological and neurological factors influencing the boys and young men around us so that we can act with greater understanding and compassion. In knowing more about boys' brains, minds and bodies we are also afforded an opportunity to better understand our own mechanisms for doing the things we do and acting the way we do. We may even save our own brains from the seemingly tiresome task of trying to figure out why boys do the things they do, and instead provide positive avenues for them to do so. If we can empathise with boys by understanding how their brains and minds work, then we can concentrate greater energies towards accommodating them in a proactive, pro-social and positive manner: they are all 'human' after all.

Exploring the humanity of boyhood is what this book is all about. The following pages offer the reader an exploration the evidence suggesting that the brains of boys operate somewhat differently to that of girls. However, prior to delving into aspects of brain difference related to sex, it is important to note a number of pertinent points. While structural and physiological differences exist between boys and girls, they also exist within each gender – it is important to note that not all male brains are exactly the same. There are, however, tendencies manifested in the general make-up of the male brain when we look at large populations of males rather than specific individuals that suggest that if we truly want to help boys succeed, we need to develop a better understanding of, and a way of accommodating for, these differences.

While embracing such a perspective, it is also important to set a contextual framework by looking at how boys operate and exist on a daily basis, for brain research also recognises the important links between the brain and the social and environmental contexts that influence behaviour and decision making.[11] An approach for working with boys that recognises differences in the male brain should not omit the equally important role the environment plays in shaping some of these differences. In particular, new research points to the significance of the environment in relation to brain plasticity and development.[12] For example, some years ago John T Richardson, a researcher in cognition and memory, argued that understanding gender differences required an acknowledgement of the relationship between life experiences and cognitive ability.[13] There are equally compelling arguments articulated across many disciplinary fields that recognise the interplay between biology, life experiences, cognition and other attributes associated with the brain and mind.[14] Indeed, we must take into account how nurture influences nature and how nature can impact the nurturing process. With all of this in mind, we can look at the male brain and the question of how we can better engage with boys using the following sections of this book.

Chapter 1 develops a framework for understanding sex differences by teasing out differences in terminologies. Sex and gender, while often used synonymously, are not exactly the same thing and it is important to understand the subtle nuances between the two. However, the case is also made that it is often convenient to refer to sex and gender synonymously and a preferred approach in this book. This then allows us to look at the biology of differences and map out aspects of 'gender' which sit on the periphery of the aims of this book.

Chapters 2 and 3 explore the brain and its development, and sex differences in the brain, respectively. The science presented in these chapters is important for shaping the ideas and strategies for Chapters 4 through 6, which focus on different aspects of nurturing the nature of boys. The nature of boys is explored through understanding the issues, challenges and opportunities related to various aspects of educating and raising boys and focuses specifically on working with boys physically, cognitively/academically, and emotionally.

After looking at ways to help boys develop, mature and grow in Chapters 4 through 6, Chapter 7 explores how to work with boys spiritually. This chapter seeks to examine how boys are often penalised for just being boys. A discussion of the mistreatment of boys is also provided in this chapter and offers the reader further insights into why, at times, the 'problematic' behaviour of boys is often in the eyes of the beholder. This is particularly important with regard to the current zeitgeist of 'toxic masculinity', whereby numerous notions of being male are brandished as detrimental to social norms and human endeavour. In a sense this important discussion is an attempt to 'counter the signals sent to boys (from society, the media, from some women who hate men, and some men who hate themselves) that being male is somehow intrinsically dirty, dangerous, inferior and/or tyrannical.[15]

The last chapter of the book then delves into how specific experiences can contribute to the developing male brain. There are specific challenges in raising and educating boys that vary from those encountered when raising girls. Meeting the needs of boys may require different approaches and a more nuanced understanding of why boys operate the way they do. The foundation for this approach is premised on neuroscientific and psychological research, and the translation of that research into various levels of discussion and practical use.

It is anticipated that this volume of ideas and its framework will be critiqued and subject to scrutiny. Readers will come to this book with their own set of beliefs about the origins and significance of gender differences. You may have certain understandings derived from personal and professional experience and as such, I ask that you consider the arguments and evidence presented with an open mind. My own ideas have changed over the years, and I have written this book with over 30 years of experience as an educationalist, 20 years as a researcher and university scholar along with my experience as a father and being male. I recognise that there may be some inherent bias in the framework presented but have tried to alleviate any bias by exploring multiple perspectives on sex and gender and providing the best evidence I could find. And the best evidence I have found acknowledges that although the fact that males and females have different brains should not be entirely surprising, it is also very controversial given that one of the implications of such a position means that not all brains think the same way and therefore not all things are equal. However, any discussion focusing on improving the lives of children should be open to analysis and debate, and this type of discourse is most welcome. Failure to acknowledge a need for critique and evaluation is antithetical to my own professional philosophy, and as neuroscientific research continues to grow, so too should the discussion on how best to meet the needs of all children through the interpretation of such research.

Finally, in writing this book, the intent was to put together a volume of work that both parents and teachers would be able to look at with a great deal of clarity. To that end, I have attempted to simplify the neuroscientific and research jargon and provide a user-friendly piece offering the right balance of theory, practical insight and useful suggestions. It is hoped that this book gives the reader insights into working with boys that are unambiguous, relevant and easily implemented, while simultaneously providing a new lens for understanding what happens when an X and Y chromosome combine. After all, the book's primary message is that in order to accept boys as human, even if we suspect the contrary, we must first adjust our perceptions of what boys truly are and how we can best work with them.

Sex and gender

'Then you should say what you mean,' the March Hare went on. 'I do,' Alice hastily replied; 'at least – at least I mean what I say – that's the same thing, you know.' 'Not the same thing a bit!' said the Hatter. 'You might just as well say that "I see what I eat" is the same thing as "I eat what I see"!'

— *Lewis Carroll,* Alice's Adventures in Wonderland

Who would have thought that the work of Lewis Carroll could be pertinent to a discussion on the terms 'sex' and 'gender'? We can even borrow Carroll's depiction of going down a rabbit hole to describe the attempt to demarcate the differences and similarities in those same terms. Indeed, when trying to set out a succinct discussion and comparison between sex and gender it can appear to be a journey that becomes increasingly strange, problematic, difficult, chaotic and complex as young Alice found out!

It is important to note from the outset that many individuals use the terms sex and gender synonymously while others insist that the two are different aspects of something similar. This has caused a great deal of confusion about the terms themselves and how they are used. This chapter begins by unpacking what the words 'sex' and 'gender' actually mean and how they have been used depending on context and agenda. This chapter also outlines how the terms are used throughout this volume of work and the reasons for such an approach. An appropriate starting point, therefore, is unpacking the meanings of each of the terms and how they are often differentiated from one another.

Are sex and gender different?

As we've noted, this is a confusing question for people, and the answer really depends on who you ask. At the time of writing this book, Google provided 329 million results to such a question. There are many reasons why this sheer volume of results exists, but perhaps one of the most prominent is that over the years the terms sex and gender have become highly political in many contexts and as such have amassed more nuanced definitions in each. However, the approach for understanding sex and gender in the context of this book is premised on the belief that sex and gender are indeed two sides of the same coin that have become blurred over time.

In its simplest sense, sex refers to the biological differences in one's anatomy and physiology that distinguish a person as male or female. Gender, while being more difficult to define, typically embraces the labels masculine and feminine to describe the role of males and females in society or an individual's conceptual framework of themselves.[1] For most people, the words sex and gender are used synonymously, but for many researchers in the area of gender studies, gender also occupies aspects of psychology, society and culture which can shape an individual's subjective sense of self, notions of masculinity and femininity and/or the cultural expectations of maleness and femaleness. And while this book adopts the synonymous use of sex and gender as a biological reality, it is important to describe why such an approach is deemed most suitable for educating and raising boys, and girls for that matter.

First, it is well established in the scientific literature that 99.98 per cent of human beings are biologically male or female: being male or female is based on having an XX (female) or XY (male) chromosomal make-up and being able to produce the reproductive cells (ovum or eggs and sperm) of that sex.[2] This objective biological fact is a truism regardless of sexual orientation or individual notions of identity. In very rare circumstances, an individual has both XX and XY cells, which can result in having components of both male and female genitalia and is now referred to as being 'intersex'.[3] This condition is extremely rare and the best estimates suggest that intersex births account for approximately two out of every 10 000 births. A teacher would need to work with 100 different students a year over 35 years to have a better than a 50 per cent chance of encountering one intersex child.[4] The rarity of this condition is compounded by the fact that the vast majority of intersex individuals do not publicly present as male **and** female, but rather adopt the gender that is more prominent biologically or physically. The intricacies of intersex are highly complex and beyond the scope of this book, but it is important to reiterate that the chances of a teacher encountering an intersex student are exceedingly rare. Parents of intersex children, however, will need to seek the appropriate professional advice to support their child given that disorders of sexual development are so rare and complex.

Second, while there are some who would suggest that gender is a social construct and as such can be 'fluid' or 'non-binary', such descriptors are premised more on subjective ideological interpretations of the influence of the environment on child development rather than on the substantive amount of scientific literature related to sex differences. In other words, there isn't any empirical proof that the social environment after birth has an effect on gender identity or sexual orientation.[5] The sex of an individual is a biological fact of our species and the misappropriation of that term under the guise of activism and egalitarianism is arguably both questionable and problematic. As noted above, 99.98 per cent of humans are either XX or XY with all of the physical and physiological attributes associated with being male and female. This is not to suggest that there aren't any differences *among* males and *among* females, but even infants are able to distinguish the sex of other infants and demonstrate typical male and female behaviours long before any measure of culture or society can exact any influence.[6] Gender is not alien to human nature, nor is it accidental or an arbitrary invention of society, but rather, is at the core of human identity.[7] And while I recognise and acknowledge that the social and cultural environment does indeed play a part in shaping the minds of boys, this does not mean that notions around the constructing of gender aren't worthy of scrutiny.

The social construction of gender

Simone de Beauvoir, a French writer, philosopher, political activist, feminist and social theorist, once asserted that a woman was not born, but rather made, suggesting that gender was a social construction.[8] While many things may be lost in translation, to read de Beauvoir's work is an interesting journey into the emergence of gender as a subject to be studied using sociological as a framework for such endeavours. In itself, her work could be characterised as somewhat 'anti-male' and perhaps that is to be expected given that when she began to construct her sociological analysis of sex and gender in 1946, times were very different for both men and women. And while this chapter is not designed to offer a protracted defence or critique of de Beauvoir's work, it is important to note that her writing, along with those of other gender theorists, was instrumental in aspects of social change and the emergence of gender theory and gender studies as academic disciplines.

Gender theory, in itself, is likely where a degree of confusion about what it means to be male and female begins. Since the 1960s, gender theory has grown into an expansive and arguably ambiguous construction of a variety of subsets of topics under the term 'gender studies'. Universities teach courses ranging from 'gender schema theory' to 'gender prediction theory' to 'gendering theory' and numerous others which share the core idea that gender is fluid and a social construct, so that being a man or a woman doesn't follow from being born male or female.[9] Such a perspective often results in calls for social change that can range on a wide continuum of overall intent and potential dangers. Recent examples include the allowing biological males to compete with biological females under the guise of equality for 'trans' individuals (more on that later). This is not to say that studies of gender cannot be helpful in some sense and, like many other types of social research, provide important narratives of human experience. However, the current political climate surrounding narratives related to gender roles, expression and identity have not only expanded the imprecise sociological descriptions associated with gender, but have made the sex and gender rabbit hole that much larger.

In an effort to stay clear of the rabbit hole noted above, this book is premised on the biology and neurobiology of sex and gender rather than sociological interpretations of gender. At the core of such an approach is a belief that schools should provide young people the tools they need to take their place in society, whatever that may be, regardless of how they may choose to express or identify themselves in a rather fluid milieu of social and cultural change. But such an approach does not negate the scientific reality that chromosomes matter. In this book, therefore, gender and sex are used interchangeably: being male or female is not something that is 'assigned' at birth but, barring the rare occurrence of being intersex, is something 'recognised' at birth. This is not to say that there isn't any degree of variation amongst each gender, but by and large there are substantive reasons why boys might behave and engage with the world in different ways than girls. These result from the interplay of genetics, biology and the environment. Understanding and adopting such a position allows us to explore ideas and strategies that will assist students in developing the tools they need to move forward in society. Nonetheless, it is also important to give some attention to notions of gender identity given the increased recognition of transgender individuals and various agendas for supporting such individuals.

Sex and gender at the margins

As noted earlier in the chapter, most individuals have a relatively unremarkable experience of being born male or female, identifying as male or female and feeling masculine or feminine within the cultural context in which they are educated and raised.[10] However, there are degrees of masculinity and femininity resulting from experience and individuals may even discuss what it means to be a man or woman during particular social and cultural contexts. Such considerations typically fall under notions of 'gender identity' and 'gender roles', concepts which are challenged and examined through the recognition of LGBTQI identities and experiences. And while that particular label might suggest some measure of collective unity, each letter in itself represents something very different from each other letter.

The 'I' in the acronym above refers to those individuals who are intersex, and as noted earlier, are representative of very rare circumstances. The L, G and B are indicative of sexual orientation – lesbian, gay and bisexual respectively. Interestingly, these categories appear reasonably stable across a population: approximately three per cent of men and one per cent of women identify as homosexual, 0.5 per cent of men and one per cent of women as bisexual and the remainder of a general population identifies as heterosexual.[11] It is important to note that sexual orientation is not the same as gender: those who identify as being gay or bisexual still acknowledge their respective biological sex as being male or female. Recent surveys conducted in times of increased societal acceptance of homosexuality and bisexuality have not shown a higher incidence of either sexual orientation.[12] In other words, whether an individual is heterosexual, homosexual or bisexual, biological sex is not a point of speculation or subjective interpretation. This, however, is not the case when discussing the remaining letters, T and Q.

Q, within the LGBTQI acronym, stands for 'queer'. The term itself is derived from postmodern and Marxist theory, and became prominent through gay liberation movements in the 1990s. It was at this time that 'queer theory' arose as a political and academic discourse and mechanism for dismantling homophobia.[13] The essence of queer theory is in the word queer, which signifies a sense of difference or strangeness, and is adopted by those individuals who desire to be seen as anything other than the 'norm'.[14] Today, to be queer can mean many things and it is often used as an umbrella term for all those in the LGTBQI community and/or as a label to identify as anything other than heterosexual or biologically male or female. As such, it is difficult to define, and is open to a variety of definitions and interpretations even in the queer community itself. However, being queer does not negate the fact that unless a person also identifies as intersex, their sex/gender/biological identity will still consist of a chromosomal make up that is either XX (female) or XY (male). This is also true of transgender individuals – the T in LGTBQI.

Transgender is an umbrella term that generally refers to individuals who experience or present and express their gender identity as incongruent to their biological sex.[15] For example, transgender individuals who are biologically male may express that they feel or identify as being female. Being transgender is a complex phenomenon and can also include individuals who identify as being not exclusively masculine or feminine ('non-binary', 'bigender', 'pangender', 'gender fluid' or 'agender') and the opposite of 'cisgender' (those whose gender identity and expression match their biological sex).[16] Currently, issues and challenges associated with being transgender appear highly politicised and as yet are not well understood by the scientific community. Histrocially, transgenderism fell under the label of having 'gender identity disorder', suggesting that individuals who felt they were trapped inside the wrong body were dealing with a psychological condition. However, there is growing evidence that being transgender might actually be linked to biology itself.

As noted above, there are an increasing number of studies suggesting that transgendered individuals neurologically relate to the sex they identify with rather than their biological sex.[17] In other words, a scientific definition of what it means to be transgender recognises that while the sex of the body is unambiguous, the sex of the brain may be decisive in determining one's sexual identity: a male brain in a female body will result in a person who feels like a man in a woman's body.[18] Such a perspective acknowledges that human brains, in themselves, can be male or female, which in turn helps build a case for different approaches to educating and raising boys and girls. This is covered in greater detail in Chapter 3, but the significance of these findings also plays a role in aspects of mental health and wellbeing. The biology of the brain clearly has profound implications for a person's sense of identity and for transgender individuals this can lead to a great degree of distress or what is referred to in psychiatric literature as gender dysphoria.[19]

It is difficult to imagine what it would be like to feel that your 'gendered' sense of self does not align with your biological self, especially when social biases may prevent such individuals from living satisfying lives. However, for teachers and parents it is important to remember that encountering students who present themselves as transgender is rare. It is very difficult to determine what percentage of the Australian population may be transgender given an unwillingness by some to self-report and by the conflation of statistics that occurs when combining all individuals within the LGTBQI community. For example, while the Australian Human Rights Commission suggested in 2014 that approximately 11 per cent of the Australian population had a diverse sexual orientation and fell under the parameter of LGTBQI, there wasn't any breakdown as to the representation of each category within that group.[20] Such statistics are undermined by other more recent studies estimating that 3.2 per cent of Australian adults identify as 'non-heterosexual.'[21] For those researchers the term 'non-heterosexual' was used to include all who identified as gay, homosexual, lesbian or those who construct their sexuality in other ways using non-heterosexual terminologies (e.g. queer). Again, the rabbit hole looms larger when one embarks on a journey of subjective interpretations of gender.

A further difficulty in attempting to determine what proportion of a population identify as transgender may lie in how being transgender is defined. For example, if you define transgender to strictly mean those who wish to transition to the opposite sex, the best estimate of prevalence is nine per 100 000 or approximately .009 per cent. However, if being transgender refers to individuals who 'feel' they are the opposite sex but do not wish to transition then the prevalence rises to 871 in 100 000 or about .871 per cent.[22] In either case, however, that number is still relatively small, and it is unlikely that most teachers will encounter a student dealing with 'actual' gender dysphoria[23] during their professional career or that the majority of parents will encounter this with their own children. This is particularly significant when considering the behaviours of young children.

Teachers and parents alike must always remember that quite often children will playfully, and with degree of childhood curiosity, pretend to be the opposite sex. Such explorations are not a sign of being transgender or refuting their biological sex, but rather the normal experimentations children may embark on as they grow and mature. Indeed, such behaviours are as common as parents who worry about those behaviours, but this type of play and exploration is a healthy sign of development whereby children are exploring who they are and also clearly delineating differences between boys and girls. Remember that children will also pretend to be superheroes, monsters and puppies but that does not mean they intend to save or terrorise the planet or spend their lives fetching sticks. Moreover, and regardless of the gender play noted above, the biological make-up of children manifested as being male or female will impact on many aspects of behaviour and learning.

Finally, while it is important to recognise that there are those who for whatever reason do not identify with their biological sex or position themselves as 'non-binary' or 'gender fluid', it is equally important to bear in mind that with the exception of about 0.02 per cent of the human population, all individuals are biologically male or female and, as such, gender identity and biological sex are not mutually exclusive. Additionally, and as alluded to in the discussion of transgender individuals above, there is substantive evidence recognising the sexually dimorphic nature of the brain or what the layperson might refer to as the existence of a 'male' and 'female' brain. It is the 'male' brain and the biological sex differences in the brain that shape the foundation of this book. These sex differences are explored in greater detail in Chapter 3, but prior to unpacking the complexities of a male brain, the next chapter provides an overview of how the brain develops in utero and through adolescence.

Summary

The complexities surrounding the terms 'sex' and 'gender' can be very confusing to most people. Today those complexities are exacerbated by a myriad of social, cultural and political agendas. In this book sex and gender are used interchangeably as the book is based on a biological framework. The following chapters are premised on the biological reality that a male possesses an X and Y chromosomal make-up and produces sperm and as such will, on average, display certain behaviours and traits resulting from their biology. For parents and teachers who find themselves working through issues of identity with any young person such matters often require assistance from professionals in mental health and wellbeing.

Understanding the developing brain

Many people think of the brain as a computational object that is programmed to make sense of incoming information and act appropriately. But contrary to the brain-as-computer metaphor, the brain does not come out of a box ready to go. It takes years of experience to build a brain – and much of this construction happens well after birth.[1]

— *Professor Sam Wang*

The human brain is a truly remarkable thing and, in many ways, still a neuroscientific mystery. There is much that we know about the brain and so much more for us to learn. This chapter explores some important aspects of what we do know, which provides the overall foundation for this book. Given the importance of understanding key aspects of the brain and its development this chapter is lengthier than the others but necessarily so. From the outset, however, let's begin by acknowledging that we still do not know a great deal about how the brain works. The brain has been an object of study for many generations and while advances in technology have provided opportunities to actually see the brain as it thinks and responds to stimuli, most neuroscientists would probably agree that we still know very little about the brain. David Eagleman most eloquently sums up this sentiment in stating that:

Of all the objects in the universe, the human brain is the most complex: There are as many neurons in the brain as there are stars in the Milky Way galaxy. So, it is no surprise that, despite the glow from recent advances in the science of the brain and mind, we still find ourselves squinting in the dark somewhat.[2]

Perhaps two of the most mysterious aspects of the brain keeping scientists squinting in the dark are emotions and intelligence.

For most people, emotions are easily displayed but sometimes not well understood. The neuroscientific literature generally refers to emotions as affective states that are a response to environmental stimuli evoking some measure of feeling. That might sound simple enough, but emotions are very complex and difficult to study. Much of what we know about the human brain comes from research with animals, particularly other mammals, and it is exceptionally difficult for neuroscientists to link human emotions, feelings and behaviour to even well-designed animal studies.[3] Moreover, when it comes to aspects of gender and emotions, the waters get even muddier, which we will explore in greater detail in Chapter 6.

Another reason for our limited understanding of affective states is that historically, neuroscientific research has focused more on the cognitive or thinking aspects of the brain and 'as interest in cognition rose, research on emotion declined in neuroscience.'[4] However, the last couple of decades have seen a significant increase in the research of human emotion, and there is a growing list of evidence available to better understand emotions.[5] These works, in turn, help to shape our understanding of working with boys emotionally in Chapter 6, but we must remember that neuroscience is only on the cusp of knowledge regarding the emotional part of the brain.

While emotions have received less attention than cognition or thinking processes in the brain, our understanding of intelligence is not that much clearer than that of emotion. The term 'intelligence' itself is often taken to mean a general aptitude and capacity for understanding and learning, often used as a descriptor for one's competence in thinking and working through various problems. But one could also ask what exactly is intelligence? The biological basis and neurological underpinnings of intelligence are highly complex and not well understood. For example, what happens in one's mind for the brain to draw conclusions, manipulate knowledge, think abstractly, simulate novelty or have a 'light bulb moment'? Neuroscientists know a great deal about where certain activity occurs and which parts of the brain perform certain roles, but to date, they have little understanding about the nature and depth of intelligence in human beings. Again, this is compounded by our inability to draw conclusions from animal studies given the unique characteristics of the human brain. While neuroscientists are able to watch the brain at work, there are still many unanswered questions as to why it does what it does and how intelligence comes to be. And if emotion and intelligence aren't complicated enough, what do we make of trying to describe the 'mind'?

Mind the mind!

In its simplest sense, the 'mind' is the brain in action. However, the mind is a somewhat ambiguous concept that is often separated into two entities, one being the neurologically determined part shaped by evolution (nature) and the other the culturally and socially determined part shaped by learning (nurture). Many researchers would argue that this is a very problematic dichotomy, for we now know that nature and nurture interact with one another and do not always work in isolation. Perhaps a more succinct portrayal of the brain and mind connection can be found in noting that:

> *Everything about our minds is the result of what happens in our brains, from the most automatic mechanisms that govern breathing to the most refined, culturally elaborated details of wedding etiquette and existential angst. That means, though, that the brain must be profoundly flexible, sensitive, and plastic and be deeply influenced by events in the outside world.*[6]

Therein lies one of the great mysteries of the mind, how much is nature and how much is nurture? Those parents with two or more children see this played out every day where, in the same home environment, children presumably housing the same genetic material can be quite different in how they engage with the people and the world around them. So, while we may have a greater understanding of how the brain might work, there is much that is still unknown about the 'mind'.

Further areas of mystery for neuroscientists include how information is stored in regions of the brain and how memory works. Again, scientists have uncovered important structural and chemical characteristics that house and influence memory, but little is known about memory retrieval or storage. For example, we don't know how the brain is capable of storing long-term memories, or and what influences how and when the brain decides to remember something. Old ideas about the brain behaving like a computer with little storage compartments for memory are being replaced with a view of the brain as an active ecosystem operating at a neural level with no single centre for memory.[7] And while research has provided some valuable insights into how we might improve our capacity to remember and what may impede memory, the fine details of how memories flow through the grey matter of our psyche are still vastly unknown.

Other areas which still puzzle the field of neuroscience include how brains sleep and dream, consciousness, when learning actually begins, how regions of the brain integrate with each other, and to what extent male and female brains differ from one another. The focus of this book is on the latter question and what this means in terms of educating and raising boys, but before we explore potential differences between boys and girls in relation to the brain, it is important to have a general understanding of how the brain develops and operates and why it has been described as the most unimaginable thing imaginable.

The human brain: imagining the unimaginable

Roughly 20 billion years ago a single point of inconceivable density and heat exploded simultaneously with equally inconceivable energy. From the dirt, dust and debris of this explosion emerged the galaxies, stars and planets that we have come to call our universe. Generally accepted as a model for the origin of the universe, the Big Bang Theory is seen as an unparalleled event defying the imagination and beyond complete comprehension. But consider this: if you were to hold a human brain in the palm of your hand, you would be holding around 1 000 trillion possible synaptic connections between nerve cells which in themselves outnumber all of the stars and planets in all of the known galaxies. In fact, there exist more possible ways to connect the neurons of a single brain than there are atoms in the universe.[8] If that seems a bit difficult to get your own head, and brain, around then think about it another way: if you wanted a computer with the same computational power as any human brain, you would need a building about a hundred stories in height and the size of the state of Texas.[9] The expanse of the universe may defy imagination but, then again, the workings of the brain are just as unimaginable. Fortunately, a moment in time not too long ago gave a great deal of impetus to humanity coming to terms with the universe residing in our skull.

On 17 July 1990 President George HW Bush signed Proclamation 6158, declaring the 1990s the 'Decade of the Brain'. This important presidential statement was not only a worldwide catalyst for the contribution of greater research dollars to neuroscience but also helped expand research between neuroscience and other discipline fields. Moreover, not unlike the first half of the twentieth century being heralded as the age of physics, the beginning of the twenty-first century became the age of brain and mind science.[10] Neuroscientists, psychologists, educators, doctors, therapists and others with professional interests in how the mind works started to delve into a reinvigorated and growing body of research focused on how the brain grows, learns and operates. Questions surrounding aspects of mental illness, cognition and learning, memory, behaviour, emotions and general wellbeing were being teased out and re-examined due to advancements in technology. Functional brain scanning started to unlock mysteries of the brain and present them to the public in many forms. Indeed, if you were to look at the number of books and articles produced since President Bush put pen to paper you would notice that this growth in reader-friendly explorations into the human mind has arguably surpassed any other era of brain-related work. Yet even after so much writing and research, it is revealing that there is so much more to know. As neuroscientist and author Joseph LeDoux has suggested, imagining the sophisticated nature of the grey matter between our ears is perhaps entirely unimaginable... but we should at least try![11]

In order to imagine the unimaginable and understand the brain it seems prudent to start from the beginning. The brain begins to from just seventeen days after conception, during the embryonic stage. The term embryo is used by medical personnel and biologists to describe these early days of development up to the end of the first trimester and then fetus is the preferred term for the remaining development in utero.[12] However, for simplicity's sake, we will use the word baby when discussing development in utero and immediately after birth.

So, what do the early stages of brain development tell us? The brain begins its amazing developmental journey very early on in a baby's life, and as such, we have become increasingly aware of the importance of health and lifestyle choices as soon as the decision to have a baby is made, or as soon as the pregnancy becomes known. Failure to recognise the significance of diet, nutrition, lifestyle and the surrounding environment simultaneously fails to recognise the potential for huge neurological repercussions given the chemical nature of the brain.

During the first couple of months, the brain will develop into two distinct hemispheres with particular areas of specialisation but a coordinated operation. Given the context of this book it is extremely important to note that all brains start out 'female'. During the first trimester, an XY (male) chromosomal make-up signals the production of male sex organs and their constituent hormones. It is these sex organs that will bombard the brain with testosterone which in turn helps carve out a male brain. In other words, some six to eight weeks in utero, and long before any sense of nurturing or acts of 'culture' can take place, nature is deciding whether the structures and mechanisms of the brain will function along a male or female trajectory. The introduction of male sex hormones on the brain will ultimately affect the timing and many other aspects of brain development.[13] This development, in turn, is linked to the proliferation of neurons.

Neurons, synaptic connections and myelin

From the first trimester to birth, the brain undergoes rapid development so that by eight months most of the baby's brain is active. In order for this to occur, it is estimated that some 250 000 neurons are generated every minute during pregnancy resulting in more than 100 billion neurons (roughly half the number of stars in our galaxy) forming before birth.[14] Neurons are brain cells and the building blocks for the brain's synaptic superhighway. Neurons differ from other cells in a number of ways, and while a single neuron is almost useless, groups of interconnected neurons transmit information to one another like elegantly complex electrochemical computers.[15] This transmission of information happens via electrochemical impulses, or what are commonly known as synapses.

A synapse occurs when any of our five senses respond to stimulation from the external or internal environment. The body parts we associate with our senses – eyes, ears, nose, tongues and skin – are continually gathering information through highly sensitive sensory receptors and translating this information into electrical signals (action potentials) which form the language of the brain.[16] When this information continually activates synaptic transmissions then these transmissions get accustomed to firing together and eventually become hardwired circuits of the mind: neurons that fire together, wire together! The wiring between neurons is arguably what makes the brain most special and there is much hardwiring to be done in utero and even more after birth.[17] For example, newborn infants have very rudimentary vision and through continued neural stimulation via seeing things, the neural highway for sight is formed.

Synapse formation begins in third trimester and while it is activated through environmental stimulation, it is also facilitated by neurotransmitters. Neurotransmitters are the chemical messengers that allow information from the dendrites of one neuron to pass through to the axon terminals of another neuron (see Figure 2.1).

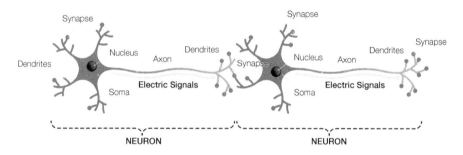

Figure 2.1 Synaptic transmissions between neurons

Neurotransmitters are detectable in the first trimester and help to stimulate growth of brain structures but become much more prolific as actual synaptic facilitators after birth. Synaptic connections are crucial in determining the longevity of a neuron: failing to make connections means that a neuron will disappear through a process known as apoptosis. While this might sound somewhat ominous, educator and researcher Patricia Wolfe notes that apoptosis is necessary to not only eliminate inactive neurons, but also 'to strengthen the connections that are left and perhaps prevent the brain from becoming "overstuffed" with its own cells'.[18]

It is through our senses and response to the environment around us that these neural connections are formed and hardwired in the brain – the more synaptic connections that occur, the greater the synaptic density and the greater the likelihood of a hardwired neural circuit. Even in utero, a baby's neurons are actively connecting as it responds to the internal environment of the womb and the external environment of its mother. Therefore, we must always remember that experience and environment help to build dendrites and neural connections.[19] There are, of course, a number of determining factors influencing neural proliferation. As Dr John Ratey from Harvard Medical School eloquently states, 'the exact web of connections among neurons at a particular moment is determined by a combination of genetic makeup, environment, the sum of experiences we have imposed on our brains and the activity we are bombarding it with now and each second into the future'.[20] Throughout the course of this book we will explore the links between boys and their experiences and environments, and how education and various aspects of raising boys may actually be out of step with male neurological development.

By the end of nine months the brain of a baby is well and truly on the way towards a phenomenal neurological process of maturation that will proceed along a developmental continuum for the next three decades. Interestingly, a baby's brain is about one third of the size of an adult brain, but its synaptic densities are nearly the same as those found in adults, and it is far more active than the brains of the adults around it. By about seven years of age, a child's brain has nearly reached the same volume as adults, but its synaptic density is still roughly 36 per cent higher because neurons actually create far more synapses with other neurons than will ever be retained in a mature adult brain.[21]

This explosion of synaptic activity after birth creates immense potential for the brain as it matures, however, it also makes a young brain somewhat inefficient and cluttered with redundant and unnecessary neural connections. Fortunately, those connections are gradually eliminated over time and most notably so during the teenage years. In a sense, the brain stockpiles neural connections during childhood and then during adolescence starts to 'prune' some of these away towards greater efficiency.

Another important aspect of brain development and efficient neural circuitry is the white matter, known as myelin, that insulates the axons of neurons. As children mature and grow, so too does the volume of myelin, which is actually what makes our brain volume increase. At the risk of oversimplification, myelin is like the protective coating found on electrical wires in that it wraps around the axons of neurons and assists in the transmission of information from one neuron to another.

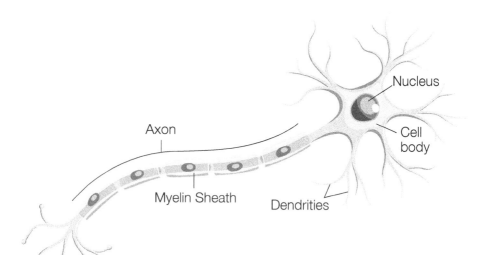

Figure 2.2 Myelin wrapped around an axon

The process of myelin build-up, or one's journey to becoming a 'fathead', is very lengthy, lasting into our twenties, and appears to develop in certain areas of the brain during certain periods of time. Some of these periods of time are critical for healthy neural development. For example, the growth of myelin coupled with visual stimulation early in life allows for the brain's visual systems to develop. There are also times that are not so critical but important in terms of learning. Researchers refer to these specific growth opportunities as 'learning windows': when the brain has greater myelinated axons in a particular region, the circuits in this region work faster and consequently there is greater neural efficiency and greater opportunity to learn. Dr Harry Chugani, one of the world's leading authorities in paediatric neurology, suggests that education systems would do well to exploit biological 'windows of opportunity', when learning is theoretically more efficient and easily retained.[22] For example, if we want children to learn a second language then they should begin doing so as early as possible rather than being forced to do so as adolescents, which is what often occurs in most schools. It is significant to note that learning windows do not ever completely close – an adult can learn to speak another language, it is just much easier to do so at an age when the brain is primed for such an endeavour. Figure 2.3 provides a graphic representation of some key learning windows and is the amalgamation of a number of works in this area.

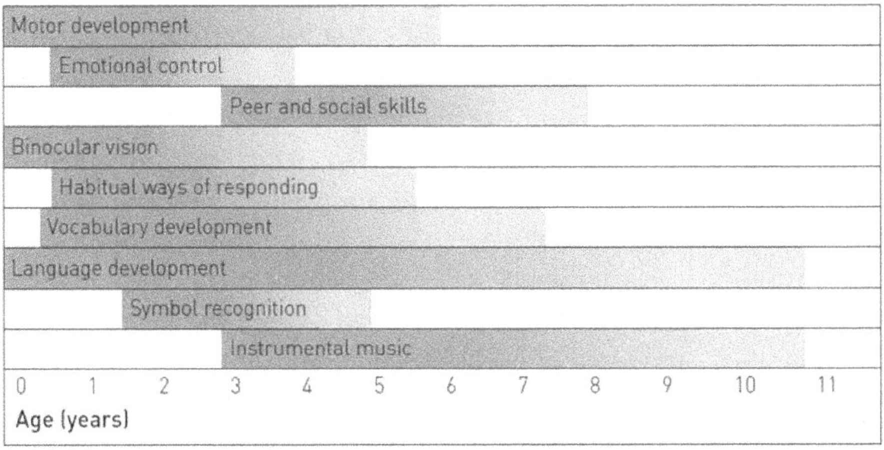

Motor development											
	Emotional control										
			Peer and social skills								
Binocular vision											
	Habitual ways of responding										
	Vocabulary development										
Language development											
		Symbol recognition									
		Instrumental music									
0	1	2	3	4	5	6	7	8	9	10	11

Age (years)

Figure 2.3 Learning windows: Key periods of neural connectivity

It is also important to recognise that the process of myelination in various neural regions is specifically purposeful in location and duration. Those axons in the brain stem and in major nerve areas running to the face, limbs, various areas of the abdomen and the organs receive substantive myelin sheaths before birth and during infancy. This allows for a baby's basic survival functions (i.e. breathing, heartbeat, seeing) to become quite efficient early in life. Concurrently, there is significant myelination in the cerebellum.

The cerebellum is a very important area of the brain. In Latin, cerebellum quite appropriately means 'little brain': it is about 11 per cent of an adult brain's weight and it has more neurons than any other part of the brain.[23] While playing a significant part in motor coordination, the cerebellum also helps to coordinate cognitive functions and thought processes as well as facilitating motor memory. Motor memory allows us to speak by manipulating our vocal chords appropriately and is also important for mental tasks like sequencing steps in long division or managing a problem.[24] Given the important contributions the cerebellum makes to our overall functioning, any deficiencies in myelin during the first two years of development would be disastrous for a child.

Finally, the areas of the brain responsible for the highest functions take the longest to myelinate. In her research work, Dr Francine Benes, director of the lab of structural neuroscience and the brain bank at McLean Hospital and Professor of psychiatry and neurology at Harvard

Medical School, found that during adolescence humans become even bigger 'fatheads'.[25] Dr Benes is a world-renowned neuroscientist specialising in schizophrenia and through her work has identified that myelin growth does not end in childhood as previously thought. Her work has shown that myelin increases up to 100 per cent in teenagers, and a male brain generally takes longer to myelinate, especially in the hippocampus and cingulate where emotion and intellect often meet. This is explored in greater detail in Chapter 6, but with all of this in mind, when does one's head actually finish myelinating? The answer to that question does vary, but a consensus seems to exist that, by and large, the brain generally continues to myelinate into a person's third decade of life. This has huge implications for boys, teachers and parents alike when coupled with other facets of brain development.

Growing, growing, gone! The developing teenage brain

An old proverb from the Pueblo peoples of New Mexico suggests that we should 'cherish youth but trust old age'. Given what neuroscience has been able to uncover regarding the maturation of the brain during adolescence, this is perhaps timeless and wise advice. Continued advances in neuroscience have changed a great proportion of the foundational tenets of psychology, cognitive science and education. For many years, it was believed that the brain was a finished product by the time a child reached 12 years of age. The work of the famous Swiss psychologist Jean Piaget had a tremendous impact on educational theory and suggested that the highest rung in the ladder of cognitive development ('formal operations' as Piaget called it) was attained somewhere around a child's twelfth birthday.[26] Contemporary neuroscientific research has now shown us that when a young person's body starts to change, his or her brain may have already begun to do so. In fact, both the grey and white matter of the brain undergo extensive structural changes well past puberty and perhaps into the mid-twenties: when puberty ends, neurological development is still occurring. Furthermore, these neurological changes can be just as dramatic as those we see when a young person's body begins to mature. Unfortunately, without the use of very expensive technology, we cannot see the brain mature in the same way as we can witness changes to the body. This often leaves us left questioning why teens might do things that would make an eight-year-old cringe in disbelief. Indeed, there are times when it seems that the teen brain goes missing as we witness changes in behaviour and attitudes that leave us dumbfounded and bewildered. These changes in behaviour, however, often serve as indicators that the teen brain is also changing!

The 'teen' brain likely begins to develop before a child's thirteenth birthday and should be linked to aspects of pubescence. Generally speaking, pubescence refers to the onset and attainment of sexual maturation and the ability to reproduce.[27] And while the teen years are often recognised as a period of transition from childhood to adulthood via pubescence and maturation, we now know that this transition includes neurological alterations.[28] These alterations can mark changes in individual behaviour which are often very dramatic and unpredictable. Interestingly, changes in brain function and maturation are equally as dramatic and often mirror teen behaviour. This helps to explain the paradoxical juncture that teen behaviour often shows – they can confront us with the physical and intellectual stature of an adult one minute and then act like a defiant and stubborn infant the next. Fortunately, the sometimes erratic, illogical and arguably irresponsible behaviour of teenagers can be better understood with reference to what is happening to the developing brain during this time.

One of the first things that springs to many people's minds when they think of the teenage years is that it is a time when hormones are raging out of control. G Stanley Hall, regarded by many as the founder of child and educational psychology, many years ago described the teenage years or adolescence as a heightened time of storm and stress, and many parents and teachers might agree.[29] Importantly, while testosterone and estrogen play a part in teenage development and behaviour, such development is far more complex than simply a sea of hormonal change. There is a complex interplay between levels of hormones and changes in the brain and as such the puzzling behaviour often witnessed during teenage years is not a singular process. There is a great deal going on in the minds and bodies of young people and it is important to recognise that understanding maturational changes associated with aspects of behaviour requires an exploration of teenage brain development that goes beyond hormonal change.[30] Such an exploration begins with a reminder of early development.

Earlier in the chapter it was noted that the brain actually goes through a process of overproduction of neural tissue. This is a central tenet in early brain development from the first trimester of life to late childhood. We are born with far more neurons then we will ever need or that are ever present in an adult brain. So, what happens to ensure that the brain is not overcrowded and inefficient? In one word ... 'adolescence'. During this time of maturation, the brain goes through a number of stages whereby it constantly remodels and restructures itself, with most of this occurring during the teenage years. It is during this time that the brain evolves along a road towards improved efficiency through a selection process often referred to using terms such as 'pruning' and 'plasticity'.[31]

As in childhood, the teenage brain is incredibly 'plastic' and shaped by the experiences around it. However, during the teenage years a substantial proportion of synaptic connections are eliminated or 'pruned', and the brain remodels itself.[32] This process is influenced by interactions with the outside world. In other words, this is a time of experience-dependent brain reorganisation where the adage of 'use it or lose it' is highly appropriate: what happens in the environment shapes the teen brain.[33] Compared to a mature adult brain, the teen brain is highly mouldable by experience. Theoretically speaking then, the educational and social environments boys are immersed in can have a direct impact on how the brain reworks its architecture. Moreover, this remodelling impacts on regions of the brain that affect everything from logic and language to impulses and intuition and is unique to this time in an individual's life.

It is easy to assume that teenage brain development is just an extension of childhood neurological development, but many of the changes that occur are unique to this period of life. This is not just a transitory stage between childhood and adulthood. It is not unusual for both a seven-year-old and a seventy-year-old to cast a puzzled look when confronted with the results of teenage decision-making. This is due, in part, to changes that occur in the frontal lobes and in the prefrontal cortex.

The prefrontal cortex forms part of the frontal lobes and sits just above the eyes, and acts as the brain's CEO. The frontal lobes are critical to controlling and monitoring planning, working memory, decision-making, mood, impulses, abstract thinking and other higher complex thinking skills. There is a plethora of evidence that much of the neural circuitry of the frontal lobes is pruned and fine-tuned during the teenage years.[34] Throughout this important region of our neural anatomy there appears to be a reduction in the volume of grey matter. Frontal lobe grey matter, which represents dense concentrations of neural tissue increases throughout childhood, peaks at around age twelve and then declines into the third decade of life. During this pruning of grey matter and unused synapses, there is also an increase in myelin production and overall neural metabolic rate which seems to indicate that the brain is in a tremendous state of flux.[35] In simpler terms, the CEO of a teenage brain is working hard one minute and then may be on holiday the next. While this occurs, acts of responsible decision-making, controlling impulses and rational behaviour can also be erratic until the brain reaches adult dimensions and maturity sometime during the third decade of life.[36] With the onset of neurological maturation, the ability to reason better, develop more control over impulses and make better judgements also matures. This pattern of growth and refinement occurring in the frontal lobes is also evident in other regions of the brain.

While there is a lot going on in the frontal lobes of a teenager, there is just as much going on in other regions of the brain. Grey matter in the parietal lobes peaks at around age eleven and then decreases through the teenage years. The parietal lobes are key players in processing sensory information and evaluating spatial relationships. The occipital lobes, which are dedicated to the processing of visual information, undergo an increase in the volume of grey matter throughout adolescence. The grey matter in the temporal lobes, which is vitally important in memory formation as well as visual and auditory processing, continues to grow until it reaches maximum volume around the age of sixteen or seventeen.[37] Needless to say, the teenage brain is undergoing an incredible transformation unmatched at any other point in a person's life. The table below offers a summary of some of the major changes in various regions of the brain during this transition into adulthood.

Table 2.1 A summary of regions of neurological change during adolescence

Brain region	Function and change
Corpus callosum	A thick bundle of nerve fibres that sits between the left and right hemispheres of the brain and facilitates communication between these two regions. For teenagers, these nerve fibres thicken and begin to process information more and more efficiently.
Nucleus accumbens	The nucleus accumbens is located in the limbic system and is part of the brain's reward system. It works in tandem with dopamine to send messages related to pleasure and sensation-seeking to the prefrontal lobes. During the teenage years this part of the brain's reward centre is engorged with dopamine and as such contributes to sensation-seeking and risky behaviour.
Hippocampus and amygdala	During childhood and adolescence, both of these areas in the limbic system increase in volume. The hippocampus has a major role in working and long-term memory storage and retrieval. The amygdala is the emotional centre of the brain and home to many primal feelings. Teenagers tend to rely more heavily on the amygdala for processing emotional information due to the restructuring of their prefrontal lobes which, when mature, is the rational thinking part of the brain. This may help to explain why teenagers act and react more impulsively than adults.

Cerebellum	As noted earlier in this chapter, the cerebellum is responsible for coordinating movement and thought processes. It helps to support higher learning like mathematics and advanced social skills, and it changes dramatically during the teenage years, increasing in nerve proliferation and synaptic complexity.
Basal ganglia	The basal ganglia work with several other structures and act like a secretary to the CEO (prefrontal lobes) by prioritising information. They also assists in regulating voluntary movements. The basal ganglia have a close connection with the prefrontal cortex and closely mirror its pattern of nerve proliferation and pruning. They also maintains a close connection with the limbic system and consequently play a role in both thinking and feeling.

Adapted from various works.[38]

In looking at the table above, one might ask why greater emphasis is not provided on each of these areas within this particular chapter. We will refer to these regions in other chapters but at this point it is pertinent to note that much of the research about the teen brain has focused on the frontal lobes and in particular the prefrontal lobes. This is due primarily to the frontal lobe's significance in all things human. If you recall, this area of the brain is the CEO of the brain, it drives a majority of cognitive processes that are unique to human beings (i.e. thinking about thinking) and is arguably responsible for so many facets of our decision-making. Of even greater interest and concern is that for all intents and purposes it is the last area to fully mature.

When we look at all of the neurological change and restructuring that occurs in teenagers, we can see that the brain actually matures from the bottom up and around to the front, which indicates that the brain stem and limbic system reach maturity sooner than areas of the cerebrum above them.[39] In other words, the parts of the brain that process sensory information with the environment (i.e. vision and hearing), coordinate those functions (fumbling with your car keys in a dark parking lot) and dictate an influx of adrenalin (fear response from the limbic system because you can't find your keys) reach maturity before the area of the brain that allows you to think through your actions rationally. The frontal lobes are the same part of the brain that teenagers use when prioritising homework and doing household chores before going to the shopping centre to hang out with friends – if they do indeed prioritise in that order! Moreover, no matter how an individual brain turns out, the maturation process remains the same, but the timing will vary from person to person.

And as we will explore in detail later, the entire process of maturation appears to occur at a different rate between males and females.[40] This is very important for both educators and parents, as it suggests that for boys and girls alike the regions of the brain responsible for survival and emotion are in full swing before the regions responsible for logical and moral reasoning can follow suit. However, a boy and girl who are the same age and perhaps in the same classroom or home environment will differ in the stages of their neurological development. This may help to explain why boys might, in some contexts, be at greater risks scholastically, socially, emotionally and even physically. Chapters 4 through 6 focus on such risks when working with boys, but the developmental timeline differences between boys and girls will have an impact on many aspects of boyhood. This becomes even more apparent in the next chapter where we look structures of the brain and sex differences within and across those structures.

Summary

The human brain is certainly an enigma wrapped in a riddle. There is so much that we do not know about it. What we do know, however, is that full development and maturation of the brain is more marathon than sprint. We also know that it is the quality and quantity of experiences we have as children and teenagers that shape much of the brain's neuro-architecture. It's important for parents and teachers to remember that the brain is a work in progress and their role is to provide the best environments possible to foster that development in a positive fashion.

3 Sex differences in the brain

Men are different from women. They are equal only in their common membership of the same species, humankind. To maintain that they are the same in aptitude, skill or behaviour is to build a society based on a biological lie.[1]

Sex influences on brain function are ubiquitous. Differences between the sexes have been documented at every level of neuroscience, from single neurons in cell culture to systems level processes as measured by neuroimaging.[2]

There is increasing evidence to suggest that the brain is a sexual organ, that brain sex is paramount in determining human gender identity.[3]

… we should come to terms with the fact that there are intrinsic neurochemical and psychobehavioral mechanisms in our brains that help create certain sex differences … it is truly remarkable how far back these differential controls go in brain evolution.[4]

The fact that males and females have different brains is not surprising, but the implication is quite important because it means that not all brains think the same way.[5]

The brains of males and females are literally wired differently, both in neuroanatomy and in neurochemistry. From studies in humans and, especially, in other animals, we know a lot about how they get that way.[6]

For many years now I have been fascinated by the growing body of evidence noting the existence of sex differences in the brain. Increasingly we are learning just how different male and female brains can be and how this may play out in the day-to-day realities of life. And while some continue to suggest that gender is predominantly a social construction and any suggestion of differences in the brains of males and females is a manifestation of 'neuro-sexism', growing scientific findings help illustrate the differences between boys and girls and how this can be, in many respects, attributed to differences in the brain. The full extent of such differences are as mysterious as some of the aspects of brain development explored in the previous chapter and as such have formed the foundations of a number of myths regarding males and females. These myths, in themselves, are worth exploring for they offer a precursor to further investigating why boys might behave and learn in very different ways than their female siblings or classmates.[7]

Myths about the brain

True or false: neurologically speaking, males and females share greater similarities than differences.

True. Currently, neuroscientific studies have demonstrated that the male and female brain share greater similarities than differences. Importantly, with each passing year greater variations between the two are uncovered and the differences that do exist are pronounced enough to have an impact on behaviour, learning, cognitive processes and many other factors shaping boys and girls, males and females. For example, on average, tests have shown that males are superior to females on a variety of spatial tasks and perform better on tests of mathematical reasoning while females are better at tasks requiring memory for the location of objects. Neuroscientists believe that this is attributable to sex differences in the brain. Moreover, while there is plenty of scientific evidence identifying sex differences in the brain much is yet to be determined regarding the full extent of these differences.[8]

True or false: the impact of sex hormones is restricted to the reproductive system.

False. Sex hormones are not only part of our reproductive system, but they also shape the neural circuitry of the brain. Moreover, sex hormones have been shown to impact numerous aspects of our affective and cognitive processing or what is more commonly known as our capacity to think, feel and act.[9]

True or false: males and females process language in the same regions of the brain.

True and false. The left hemisphere of the brain appears to do most of the work with regards to the processing of language. However, while language is lateralised in the left hemisphere for the male brain, the female brain also engages both the left and right hemisphere. There also appears to be a number of other important aspects of language processing that vary between males and females.[10]

True or false: males and females share equal attributes in terms of performing one or more tasks.

False. Numerous studies suggest that males are not as good as females at multitasking. It appears that females use greater regions of the brain than men when performing particular tasks and as such neuroscientists believe that this assists in a woman's ability to attend to a number of stimuli and shift focus on a range of things at one time.[11] It is noteworthy that findings in this area are somewhat inconclusive given the vast array of tasks any one individual may attend to at any time and our understanding of multitasking may be changing due to the omnipotence of technology and the demands of screen devices.

True or false: boys and girls are equally represented in terms of learning difficulties.

False. By and large most genuine learning difficulties appear in boys.[12] There is a great deal of speculation as to why this might be, and research continues to look at the formation of the male brain in utero and the band of tissue connecting the hemispheres of the brain (corpus callosum) for possible answers. This is not to say that girls do not present learning difficulties at all. However, many of the types of difficulties associated with behaviour and learning such as Attention Deficit Hyperactivity Disorder (ADHD) manifest differently in girls while the vast majority of challenges associated with learning difficulties are linked to boys.

True or false: the brain is fully developed structurally by the time a child reaches puberty.

False. There once was a time when it was believed that the brain's maturational journey ended around the twelfth birthday. Research now tells us that the brain continues to change and evolve well into the teens and beyond and that this process follows different developmental timelines for boys and girls. Moreover, there is a growing body of research suggesting that given the brain's 'plastic' nature we can continue to shape our neural architecture at a cellular level throughout our lives.

True or false: oxytocin, a hormone that promotes bonding, works differently and is much more functionally present in females.

True ... until later in life! Oxytocin is linked to the pleasure centres of the brain that produce natural opiates (endorphin is a good example). Both males and females have oxytocin but males are not endowed with the same number of oxytocinergic circuits in the brain and there is a significant difference in how this chemical works in men and women primarily due to how it combines with other sex hormones. For females oxytocin is responsible for social bonding ... think girls needing to hug when they see each other. For males, oxytocin in certain brain areas promotes sexual arousal, a different type of bonding! Interestingly, this appears to change with age; as males grow older, testosterone declines and male bonding behaviours resemble those of females due to the increased influence of oxytocin.[13]

True or false: in most cases, the female brain matures earlier than the male brain.

True. The rate of maturation will vary among same sex groups, but the newest research tells us that the female brain matures earlier, with most of the work completed in the early twenties whereas the male brain does not appear to complete the maturation process until the late twenties. The rate of maturation in particular areas of the brain has also been shown to impact on various cognitive abilities as well as emotional attributes.[14]

True or false: the female brain is capable of better cross-talk between the hemispheres.

True. The male brain is physically larger than the female brain yet the corpus callosum (the band of tissue connecting the hemispheres) is the same size. In essence this means that the corpus callosum is proportionally larger in a female. It also appears that the female brain has greater neural density in the corpus callosum, theoretically allowing the hemispheres of her brain to communicate more efficiently.[15]

True or false: developmental timelines for boys and girls are more similar than different.

True and false. This question is perhaps more a matter of perspective regarding how one defines 'similar'. In many respects, girls reach physical maturation ahead of boys and they also demonstrate greater maturity in terms of language ability and emotion. The difference in these timelines can be as much as six to twenty-four months depending on which attribute one is observing. As noted above however, neurological timelines suggest that the female brain matures both incrementally and holistically sooner than the male brain.

From the information presented in the myths above it should be apparent that in coming to some understanding of the human brain in general, and the male brain in particular, neuroscience has provided many answers and equally as many questions. Concurrently, when it comes to looking at and discussing any possible aspects of difference in attributes, skills, behaviour and learning according to gender, there can often be heated debate regarding such an endeavour. This is especially true when we look at gender differences in the human brain. Most people would have little difficulty believing or verifying that:

- female hearts typically beat faster than those of males, even during times of rest.
- males and females metabolise drugs differently.
- males and females display observable differences in body shape, strength and many other physical characteristics.
- smoking damages a specific gene in females and as such female smokers are four times more likely than males to die of cancer.
- stomach bile has a different composition in males as compared to females.
- male stomachs empty quicker than females.
- males generally have larger body mass, greater bone density, different muscular structures, broader shoulders and greater physical strength.[16]

So why is it that when we look at the brain, controversy arises? Perhaps the reason for this can be found in history. When we look back in time, there is ample evidence of science being misused to disadvantage some people. For example, physicians in the nineteenth century claimed that because the physical size of a woman's brain was smaller than that of a man, she had diminished capacities and intellectual abilities in comparison to her male counterpart. In other words, a woman was not as smart as a man! Beliefs and rhetoric surrounding notions of inferior biology have also used to deny many aspects of equal opportunity.[17] Understandably then, there has been much scepticism and caution when entertaining neurological differences between men and women, for such explorations can quickly be used to infer some degree of superiority of one sex over another. As such, sex differences in the brain can become an emotionally charged topic that is often left cautiously on the periphery of any discussion related to children and education. However, in the context of educating and raising happy and healthy boys, and in an era of increasing technological and scientific know-how, scepticism cannot deny the fact that there are a number of differences, across a number of regions, systems and structures in the brains of boys and girls. It is important to note, however, that males and females share many similarities and a male brain has some of the same hormones and characteristics as its female counterpart and vice versa. Some researchers have shown, via various scanning technologies, for example, that some females and males have brains that appear to 'bridge' the gender divide and therefore are somewhat atypical.[18] University of Cambridge neuroscientist Professor Simon Baron-Cohen estimates that one in seven males and one in five females are 'bridge brained' or in the middle of the sex/brain spectrum.[19] Perhaps the best description of this phenomenon in terms of understanding boys and girls comes from the work of author and researcher Dr Michael Gurian where he notes that:

> *Brain development is best understood as a spectrum of development ... many of the children you have contact with lean toward the female on the brain development spectrum, many toward the male. Mainly, your girls lean toward the female and boys toward the male, but you may also notice a number of 'bridge brains'. These are boys and girls who possess nearly equal qualities of both male and female brains.*[20]

In real-life terms, this means that we may see some girls who behave or act more like boys (tomboys) and some boys may appear more verbal or display other traits more often seen in girls, but if we are biologically male, we tend to be more male in how we engage with the world, behave and learn. Moreover, while we might agree that there exist greater similarities in neurological structure and function between the genders, we cannot disregard those areas that are different and consequently lend themselves to affecting emotion, cognition and behaviour. Contemporary science is quick to note that while there are no significant differences in overall intelligence between males and females and that neurological differences between males and females may appear tiny, they are no less real than other, more easily seen gender attributes.[21] Therefore, when we start looking at neurological structures, functions, chemicals and maturation we begin to see that treating boys and girls identically in terms of how they are raised and educated is not in the interests of either sex.

Snakes, snails and puppy dog tails ... just what are boys' brains made of?

Men are different from women and, accordingly, boys are different from girls. While this is an obvious statement, in the last few decades some of the scientific evidence acknowledging sex differences in relation to the brain has been quietly understated, for understandable social reasons we have already touched on. But in the context of educating and raising boys, neglecting these differences, or unthinkingly dismissing them under the misguided folklore that 'boys will be boys', risks missing the opportunity to meet the unique needs of boys that arise from their biological and neurological tendencies. As a species, we share the same sexual identity and neurophysiology for only a few weeks after conception. Thereafter, testosterone does its thing!

As noted in Chapter 2, roughly seventeen days after conception the brain begins to form, and in fact all brains start out female. About six to eight weeks later, testosterone can change the nature of that developmental trajectory.[22] If the baby is a female (genetically XX) then the reproductive mechanisms produce no significant amount of this predominantly male hormone. If, on the other hand, the baby is male, his brain will be exposed to massive doses of testosterone (about four times the level experienced through infancy and childhood) via the formation of his testes. Since the natural patterning of the female brain does not appear to undergo as drastic a change as the patterning of the male brain, some researchers suggest that this may be why boys are more likely to have any number of problems associated with the brain and learning: there is so much going on in the brain of a male during the first trimester of life that the opportunities for something going wrong are greater. As Professor Robert Nadeau of George Mason University clearly states:

> Since a fetus becomes male as a result of the delicate action of sex hormones on control and regulatory genes at several critical points in prenatal development, there is a greater prospect that something will go wrong. More male than female fetuses are spontaneously aborted, and males suffer far more birth defects. Male babies are also plagued by higher rates of cognitive and behavioral disorders and are 30 per cent more likely to die in the first few months of life.[23]

While testosterone is an important factor in early neural development, a growing body of research suggests that the brain is also influenced by other hormonal factors including the proportional mix of estrogen and testosterone.[24] The complexities surrounding the chemical make-up of the body and mind in conjunction with genetics reminds us that just because two boys have the same exposure to androgens prenatally does not mean they will be exactly the same – the interacting nature of other biological influences will produce differences within boys. Therefore, on the fateful day that a young boy arrives into this world, while we anticipate his neurological make-up to be 'male', we must remember this is a biological tendency, not a rule and there can be subtle differences among boys. However, the differences between boys and girls are far more pronounced and observable.

While we know a great deal about the differences between the male and female brain, neuroscience continues to grapple with the intricacies of these differences and their overall influence on brain function. However, it should be both important and exciting for parents and educators to know that some of the things boys do or say may be linked directly to what is going on inside their heads while they grow and develop. With that in mind, the remainder of this chapter will examine three important differences that have been intuitively understood for decades but are now supported by neuroscience. These differences are by no means exhaustive, but rather representative of factors that exacerbate a mismatch between raising and schooling boys and their underlying behavioural tendencies. Throughout this book these differences, along with others, will be highlighted in terms of the interplay of nature and nurture and how we might effectively accommodate boys in proactive and beneficial ways.

Male brains present male challenges!

The previous chapter provided an exploration of the brain and mind along with a fairly detailed account of current understandings of brain development from birth through adolescence. For the most part, the pattern of brain development is very similar in boys and girls, but the timing and stages of this process are different. Research consistently shows that all aspects of brain development generally occur earlier for girls than boys.[25] Ironically, while the brains of females mature earlier, many parts of the male brain actually age quicker.[26] Brain development is probably best thought of as a process lasting from early periods of prenatal life through adolescence and into old age that varies for different regions at different times and affects different behaviours.[27] This long-term developmental schedule also parallels relationships between brain development, brain function and the levels of various hormones.[28] Given these differences in developmental timelines between boys and girls, a one-size-fits-all approach to raising and educating children can therefore be problematic. For boys, an example of this is observable in the early years of life and schooling.

One of the first notable developmental differences between male and female brains is seen in language development. Girls, on average, speak earlier and better than boys, produce longer sentences and also tend to have larger working vocabularies at very young ages.[29] These differences appear to transcend the influence of nurture, as they are found to be universal across cultures.[30] Moreover, brain imaging studies continue to point to biological explanations of gender differences in language development. For example, one study found gender differences in children and adolescents in regions of the brain associated with the efficiency of processing semantic, visual and auditory information related to language. In layperson's terms, this suggests that by virtue of their brain structure and functioning, girls have an innate advantage in language development that will manifest in reading and writing skills.[31] Fortunately, most of these developmental differences appear to diminish with age, at least in terms of their influence on some aspects of academic performance. However, while many boys begin catching up with girls later in school, girls generally outperform boys on spelling, capitalisation, punctuation, language usage and reading comprehension tests. Indeed, even as adults, women tend to do better on tests of verbal fluency and other related language tasks.[32]

We must remember that any data that identifies problems boys face with language represents the *average* abilities of boys and girls. There are boys who excel at language tasks and girls who have difficulty with language or are slow to develop, but these are the exceptions, not the rule, and in spite of the boys who do well, there does appear to be a developmental delay for most boys' language skills. The end result of this maturational process is that girls tend to have an early advantage in communication and a distinct advantage in the early years of schooling where language proficiency becomes increasingly significant for learning to read and write. Reading is something that grows out of spoken language and, as noted above, boys are typically slower to begin talking and achieve the phonological awareness that plays a critical role in learning to read.[33] Therefore, school curriculum may be inherently disadvantageous for many boys if schools do not recognise and adequately accommodate the fact that the neural architecture for oral language, and by association aspects of literacy, matures earlier in girls. This is particularly problematic when it comes to labelling boys as having learning problems or pushing materials they are not developmentally ready for.

Indeed, the vast majority of students identified as having language and literacy problems requiring remedial support are boys. Given the stigma often associated with having a learning 'problem', the underlying neurological maturation timeline that leads to developmental differences in language between boys and girls needs more attention, to ensure that a boy with early literacy problems is supported in the class with developmentally appropriate material and not tagged as a student needing learning or remedial support. All students need learning support; it is the nature of education. There is, however, a difference between genuine learning difficulties and those challenges associated with chronological attributes. Moreover, when boys need to engage in school-based printed materials they are often forced to do so based on age and not their level of development: many parents have experienced being told that their sons should be reading and writing at a particular *age* level but that age level is not gender specific. It is highly likely that reading and other milestones will vary between boys and girls in the early years of schooling. The end result of this for many boys is that reading becomes frustrating, tiresome and something worth avoiding. Fortunately, boys tend to catch up with their female counterparts at about the age of eight when growth spurts in the areas of their brains that are responsible for language, memory and decision-making occurs at a rapid rate.[34]

But what exactly are the nature of the differences in the male brain that lead to this divergence in language development between boys and girls?. There are some interesting structural and functional differences that may have an impact on language development that are worthy of speculation – speculation because the neural basis for sex differences in language is only beginning to be understood. While they are speculative, they are certainly worth knowing.

One of the most striking differences noted by many researchers is the degree to which boys favour the left hemisphere of their brains. A growing body of research confirms that the left and right hemispheres of the brain are, to some extent, dominant or lateralised for different cognitive functions.[35] It is only in humans that the brain hemispheres differ significantly in structure and function, and language appears to be our most lateralised function.[36] While neither hemisphere is completely responsible for language itself or any other particular function, it appears that brain function related to most aspects of language in males tends to be more lateralised in the left hemisphere whereas language functions in females tend to be more equally distributed between both hemispheres.[37] Furthermore, the dominant language areas of the brain located in the left hemisphere actually mature earlier in girls.

MRI and PET scans both demonstrate these sex differences, with scans showing that language tends to be more localised in the left hemisphere of males. Medical research has demonstrated that women are considerably less likely to lose language function than men when they suffer a stroke or other types of brain damage to the left hemisphere; the brain of a woman will compensate for any language impairment due to the fact that the right hemisphere is already doing a good part of the job.[38] The cross lateralisation of language is representative of many processes in the female brain, which in part is due to the structure that connects each hemisphere known as the *corpus callosum*.

The corpus callosum is a band of myelinated axons that acts as a bridge between the thinking areas of each hemisphere and allows for the expeditious flow of information from one hemisphere to the other; it is, essentially, the conduit that contains the vast majority of the wiring between the hemispheres.[39]

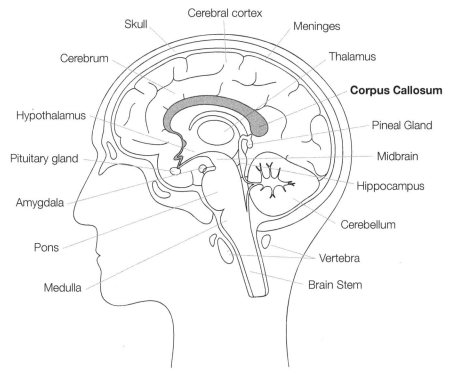

Figure 3.1 Corpus callosum

Estimates put the number of fibres in the corpus callosum between 200 and 800 million. Not surprisingly, the greater the number of connections between the hemispheres via the corpus callosum, the greater the likelihood of better language and other associated functions.[40] In females, the corpus callosum appears proportionally larger and more bulbous than in males, and is also synaptically denser, indicating more and potentially stronger connections between the hemispheres.[41] Whether a greater sharing of function between hemispheres through the corpus callosum is an advantage or not generally depends on the cognitive function in question, but for language, the evidence appears to speak for itself. Women typically have higher verbal IQs, greater proficiency in a range of language-related tasks and abilities, superior verbal fluency and the ability to compensate for any damage to the left hemisphere.[42]

In addition to the lateralisation of language between the brain's left and right hemispheres, there exist two other important regions of the brain that mediate language and are proportionally larger in females than males. Broca's area, named after French neurologist Paul Broca, is the area of the brain that helps to produce fluent spoken and written language; it is the grammatical and syntactic centre for putting language together in a coherent fashion. Wernicke's area, named after German neurologist Carl Wernicke, is the region of the brain that helps to process specific elements of language; it is the place where language is understood. Both of these important language regions are responsible for other activities, and in addition to being proportionally larger in females, close analysis of Wernicke's area in women has identified that the neurons in this region are more densely packed together and have longer dendrites than those of men.[43] If we remember the importance of neurons and dendrites outlined in Chapter 2, then it stands to reason that thicker neural density and greater neural connectivity equals greater proficiency. In other words, a girl will generally have greater expertise and ability in the verbal arena due to how language abilities are hardwired in her brain.

In practical terms, the research regarding the structures and functions critical to language development suggests that current educational settings where children begin their literacy education at the young age of four or five may not be doing much good for many boys. Moreover, a teacher who is unaware of this and continues to work with boys in the same manner as working with girls may not be doing the male brain any favours – this is explored in greater detail in Chapter 5. On a broader spectrum, educational contexts where boys' and girls' literacy skills are developed in the same fashion, with the same curricula, assessment tools and pedagogical approach, may be culpable in the number of boys who leave school with substandard literacy levels.[44] How boys engage with language and the world of literacy requires differentiation in approach, expectation and content. Perhaps, as research continues to advance, time will tell how accurate these assertions might be. In the meantime, an examination of the role of serotonin and testosterone may also prompt some concern for how we raise and educate boys.

Serotonin and testosterone – a perfect male storm!

In Chapter 2 we briefly explored the role of neurotransmitters – the chemicals that facilitate communication between neurons and affect the activity, maintenance and longevity of synapses and neurons themselves. Commonly known chemical messengers include serotonin and dopamine. Each of these helps to send inhibitory or excitatory messages, and each fluctuates in intensity and duration depending on environmental stimuli. In other words, an individual's response to the environment around them and their experiences will affect their levels of various neurotransmitters, which in turn influences the brain and by association behaviour and learning. Dopamine receives greater attention later but by way of an example, let's briefly look at how serotonin might impact upon the behaviour of a boy.

Serotonin has received a great deal of research attention over the last decade and is a very important brain chemical for it acts as the brain's great inhibitor in the areas that control motivation and emotional behaviour. It also carries out communication in and between the brain and body, and is linked primarily with processing emotions and acting as a calming mechanism. Serotonin also plays a role in the control of eating, sleeping and arousal, as well as the regulation of pain and various moods. Serotonin stops us from doing things – it helps to tell us when we are not hungry anymore, when we are feeling tired, and most importantly, it curbs impulsive behaviour. There are also specific neural circuits in the brain that are governed by serotonin. These circuits help to link the limbic system (emotion) with the frontal lobes (the brain's thinking centre) and these two areas can be in conflict when emotive impulses want to override the rational thought.

The importance of serotonin cannot be understated, for it is the neural pathways facilitated by serotonin that help keep emotions and impulses from running wild.[45] Researchers associate high levels of serotonin with high self-esteem and social status while low levels of serotonin have been linked with impulsivity, risky behaviour, anger and hostility.[46] J John Mann of the Columbia Presbyterian Medical Centre even goes as far as citing research evidence linking low levels of serotonin with suicidal tendencies.[47]

A couple of key points for educators to consider regarding serotonin is that stress, especially chronic stress, can inhibit the brain's production of serotonin and simultaneously impair the cognitive functions of the prefrontal cortex.[48] Second, while both males and females have serotonin, males do not appear to process it as efficiently as females which can impact on their behaviour.[49] Levels of serotonin and dopamine have been linked to impulsive and fidgety behaviour which can present itself clinically as Attention Deficit Hyperactivity Disorder (ADHD), a condition found mostly in males and arguably over-diagnosed in boys.[50] Moreover, it appears that levels of serotonin in the brain may also decline temporarily during adolescence.[51]

The full complexity of serotonin's role in behaviour is beyond the scope of this book, but on face value the research suggests that the fidgety and impulsive tendencies of boys may be linked to the levels and processing of serotonin and other neurotransmitters. Many boys may be chastised for an inability to sit still or calm down when they are only engaging with the world in a way that is innate to them due to the chemical milieu of their brains. This is not to say that we should excuse unacceptable behaviours as a product of invisible chemical reactions, but we also should not condemn boys when they find it difficult to sit still and stay on task. Indeed, for parents and educators, all of the factors noted above should be important considerations in how we deal with boys and indeed all students across any year level. Asking a fidgeting boy to stop squirming during class discussions might be as successful as asking that same boy to hiccup on demand. Furthermore, all adults would do well to consider that children who are stressed are students whose ability to learn may be impeded, but this may be even more critical to remember during adolescence when serotonin levels fluctuate further. Couple this with increasing recognition that efficient and constructive learning cannot take place when a learner is experiencing fear or stress and it becomes imperative that educators begin to consider that contexts of underachievement and inappropriate behaviour at school may be symptomatic of physiological and neurological processes. This becomes increasingly important when considering how testosterone may further disadvantage boys in an educational context.

Most of us recognise testosterone as the male growth hormone. We also know that it is often linked with aggressive behaviour. Author and former principal of a prestigious Australian boys school Dr Tim Hawkes suggests that while aggression is a product of many factors, there is little denying the significant role testosterone plays in exacerbating a predisposition for aggressive behaviour in boys.[52] There is a plethora of animal and human studies that support Dr Hawkes' assertions, and also show that the range of aggressive behaviours in males will vary in relation to levels of testosterone.[53] However, what does not vary is that boys will experience great surges in testosterone levels at various stages throughout their lives.

Early in a boy's life, cellular development in certain cortical regions of the brain is slowed by testosterone. Research has also demonstrated that various aspects of synaptic formation and pruning may also be slowed in boys by testosterone during early postnatal development. Testosterone has been shown to have an impact on visual acuity, the olfactory system and the myelination of neurons in the auditory cortex.[54] In all of these aspects of the brain, and as with regions of the brain associated with language development, boys tend to mature and develop somewhat later than girls, but fortunately much of this occurs early enough in a boy's life so as to limit its long-term impact in educational contexts. However, as boys grow older and when puberty arrives, testosterone can directly influence the day-to-day circumstances of boyhood in schools.

A boy will experience various stages of testosterone surges throughout his life. Somewhere around the age of ten, these surges occur more frequently and can make a boy's mood vacillate from being aggressive to being withdrawn.[55] High levels of testosterone exacerbate aggressive behaviour and a desire to be active, while low levels see boys make behavioural shifts towards apathy and introversion. Furthermore, the behaviours and moods of boys are very dependent on the interplay of neurotransmitters and hormones. The impact of testosterone and serotonin in the minds of boys has tremendous implications for parents and educators. For example, an approach to education that continues to insist its participants are sedentary and relatively inactive for long periods of time is not the best way to counteract impulsivity or a predisposition for movement resulting from a cocktail of hormones and neurotransmitters. Nor is a prolonged home diet of inactivity due to excessive screen time helpful in raising healthy young men. In Chapter 4, where we look at strategies for working with boys physically, we explore the importance of movement for boys and why boys should spend more time outside. In the meantime, we can detail one other aspect of difference between a boy's and a girl's brain by looking at the limbic system and the interplay of emotion and behaviour.

Martians, Venusians and emotions

In 1992, Dr John Gray released a book that became a bestseller and fodder for talk show hosts, comedians, life coaches and relationship gurus. While there are not fifty shades of anything in Gray's book, *Men are from Mars, women are from Venus* continues to intrigue and entertain generations of new readers trying to identify why relationships between men and women can often be so problematic. Some of the newest research available actually helps to identify a neurological basis for Dr Gray's entertaining psychological approach. Indeed, there are few who would dispute that males and females differ in emotional style and social responsiveness, and neuroscience continues to identify what many intuitively know – that when it comes to emotion men and women may as well be from other planets. Much of this is due to differences in how the limbic system operates in males and females.

As identified in Chapter 1, the frontal lobes of the brain are often referred to as the brain's CEO. If the frontal lobes are the CEO, then the limbic system could be considered the 'heart' of the organisation. Nestled in the middle of the brain just above the brain stem, the limbic system is the emotional part of the brain (See Figure 3.2). In addition, the limbic system is also a key player in memory formation, processing long-term memories, and connects the lower regions of the brain responsible for motor and automatic functions with higher regions responsible for cognition and thought.

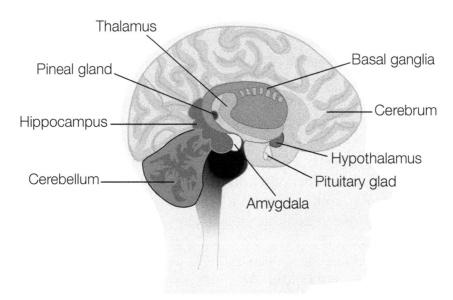

Figure 3.2 The limbic system

When fully developed, the limbic system represents about one-fifth of the brain's total volume and beyond its role in emotion and memory formation, various parts of the limbic system play a part in our sleep patterns, attention, motivation, hormones, the production of most chemicals found in the brain, the regulation of bodily functions and the initiation of the numerous appetites and urges that direct our behaviour in various ways.[56] The limbic system also drives our responses to various stimuli – it regulates our moods and physiological responsiveness to various situations and in many circumstances can actually shut down thinking. There can be no denying the importance of the limbic system. Equally, the research available also acknowledges that there is no denying that men and women differ in how they process emotion, how they perceive emotionally evocative cues, how they express emotion and how their respective brains activate various limbic structures.[57] There is also evidence of these differences in children from a very young age, which has implications for how we work with both boys and girls.

As noted in Chapter 2, testosterone helps to shape the gender architecture of the brain, which in turn will impact on the timing of brain development. One of the first differences observable between boys and girls is related to emotion and learning, and occurs in utero. In 1925, Dr Albrecht Peiper, a Leipzig University pediatrician, conducted a series of experiments to determine whether or not a baby could hear while still in the uterus. Peiper found that not only could they hear but they also formed memories through a process now referred to as 'habituation'. 'Habituation' is an element of learning in which the repeated exposure to a particular stimulus decreases the strength of a response. Simply stated, the brain will recognise a repeated non-threatening or seemingly unimportant stimulus and ignore it.[58] Peiper's discovery came as a result of monitoring fetal movement by visually confirming a prenatal response to outside stimuli through observing distension from kicking in the maternal abdomen after an automobile horn was sounded.[59] While somewhat crude in approach, his research is now verifiable via ultrasound and fetal heartrate monitors, which have confirmed that fetuses begin to respond to sounds at around five months of age. Interestingly, habituation appears earlier in girls than in boys, helping to identify that from very early in life, a girl's neural system is on an earlier developmental schedule.[60]

A further consideration related to the emotional development of boys and evident during foetal development is the impact of maternal stress on the growing foetus. Researchers have identified that high levels of maternal anxiety or stress can result in the over-production of stress-related hormones that can be passed directly to the child. During the latter part of pregnancy, the impact of excessive maternal stress has been identified through the behavioural and emotional problems in male newborns who are often fussier, more irritable and delayed in their mental and motor development.[61] In boys, the effects of an overly stressed mother manifest themselves through behaviour associated with hyperactivity and inattention. Of significance here is that almost all childhood maladies are more common in boys, including Autism Spectrum Disorder (ASD), dyslexia, learning disabilities, ADHD and Tourette's syndrome. This is not to say that a mother's anxiety is necessarily a causal link to the variety of problems a boy might face, but rather it is important to note that even in the earliest days of growth and development, the male brain is susceptible to behavioural and emotional difficulties. As boys grow older we also see greater variability in how boys and girls manage and process emotion.

Over the last decade, a number of studies have documented that male and female limbic systems maintain differences in structure and function, and that many of these differences are innate due to the fact that they emerge too early in life to be associated with nurturing.[62] As noted in Chapter 1, female infants as young as one to three days old respond with greater frequency and attention to various social stimuli including a human voice or face, while infant boys focus on objects and things.[63] Girls also make eye contact sooner and for longer periods of time, demonstrate empathy sooner, and by the age of four are better at recognising facial expressions and reading the emotional signs associated with various facial gestures.[64] Of note, however, is that while girls seem to have an advantage in terms of emotional responsiveness, boys may, in fact, be more emotional and emotionally vulnerable. Infant boys tend to startle more easily, grimace more, act more irritable and are more difficult to console.[65] As they grow older, challenges for boys in relation to sex differences in the limbic system appear to become more pronounced as females exhibit greater abilities in reading facial expressions, differentiating tones of voice for emotional nuance and an array of other capacities linked to emotional intelligence.[66]

The processing of emotion is an area of research that is still rather nascent in comparison to other neuroscientific arenas, but while there is much to be learned, much research so far suggests that females tend to be much more efficient at processing and dealing with their own emotions as well as the emotions of others. In his groundbreaking work, *The essential difference: The truth about the male and female brain*, Professor Simon Baron-Cohen of Cambridge University describes how the female brain is predominantly hardwired for empathy and emotion and therefore better at dealing with emotion and emotive responses.[67] He notes that the amygdala of boys and girls show a different pattern of responsiveness to emotive stimuli, and how structural differences in the corpus callosum and massa intermedia (an area which connects the two sides of the thalamus) allow for better overall processing of emotion in the female brain. Baron-Cohen's work has been supported by a growing body of studies identifying that males and females process and express emotions differently and has been complemented by other researchers interested in sex differences in the brain.[68]

Dr Leonard Sax goes a bit further than Professor Baron-Cohen in terms of describing why boys have problems processing emotion. As discussed earlier, the amygdala is a very important component of the limbic system and it literally adds a positive or negative tag to the memory of an emotional experience. As girls mature, a larger fraction of the brain activity associated with negative emotions shifts from the amygdala to the cerebral cortex (the area of the brain associated with higher order cognitive functions). Therefore, on or around her seventeenth birthday, a young woman is able to use the area of her brain responsible for reflection, reasoning and language as a mechanism for regulating and articulating her feelings and emotional status. This shift, however, does not happen for boys and the locus of brain activity for negative emotion remains in the amygdala. Therefore, asking a teenage boy why he is feeling down or depressed is doomed to fail. Dr Sax notes that emotions, positive or negative, are processed differently in boys' and girls' brains and that 'in boys, as in men, the part of the brain where emotions happen is not well connected to the part of the brain where verbal processing and speech happens – unlike the situation in teenage girls and in women.'[69]

Given the difficulties the male brain has in processing and articulating emotion, there can be little denying the potential for aggravating an emotive situation when a boy finds himself in some form of strife or conflict in school. All too often a boy's behaviour is misread as arrogant, stubborn or introverted when in fact his ability to describe his feelings or actions is not immediately accessible. Moreover, a boy who comes to school after being involved in some form of stress or emotional upheaval may take some time before the cognitive areas of his brain override the emotions that seemingly derail learning. Again, not being armed with this sort of information leaves educators without the requisite insight to counteract a boy's emotional difficulties and opens the potential for mislabelling a boy's lack of engagement in learning or his reaction to an emotive situation as a behaviourial issue. Later in Chapter 6, we explore strategies for working with a boy's emotions in a proactive fashion that is responsive to a boy's neural architecture. For now, we'll conclude this chapter with an overview of the structural differences in boys' brains that have been identified through research. This information is then used to highlight how teachers and parents might change their perceptions of a boy's behaviour and move towards strategies that are both advantageous for boys and responsive to what might be going on inside their heads.

My brain is bigger than yours: further neural differences!

Perhaps the first and most easily recognisable structural difference between male and female brains is size. The male brain is larger than the female brain. At birth, a boy's brain is already twelve per cent heavier and two per cent larger in circumference than a girl's brain. As children grow and mature into adults, brain size and mass generally parallel that of body size: men are generally larger than women and thus tend to have bigger brains.[70] However, this is not indicative of any measure of superiority in cognitive ability and may in fact be one of the reasons boys appear more susceptible than girls to various developmental and cognitive disorders.[71] In this sense, bigger is certainly not better! Indeed, there is no evidence to suggest that larger brains are, in any way, better than smaller brains.[72] On the contrary, in many respects the smaller female brain appears to be more efficient.

As noted earlier, the corpus callosum in females has a greater number of connections between the two hemispheres of the brain. The female brain also appears to have a greater volume of grey matter in certain regions and more extensive and intricate communications between brain cells, particularly in the prefrontal cortex. There is also a faster rate of blood flow in the female brain and some scientists believe that this is a direct result of the intricate web of neural connections found in the female brain.[73] The flow of blood to the brain is an important consideration, as the brain requires a great deal of energy, and this energy is derived from glucose which is metabolised from the nutrients in the bloodstream. Interestingly, just when boys need that extra energy due to the size of their brains, they typically have significantly lower heart rates and lower body temperatures, which in turn affects blood flow resulting in a neural energy deficit.[74]

As well as blood flow, there are other functional differences between a male and female brain. Synaptic pruning, as discussed in the previous chapter, is a very important developmental stage for the human brain. The role of hormones during synaptic pruning is equally important and various studies focusing on neural maturation tell us that major differences exist in when boys and girls prune and expand the connections in their brains.[75] This discrepancy in the schedule of synaptic pruning is another reason why developmental timelines and emotional maturity can vary significantly between boys and girls.

While brain size and synaptic pruning offer examples of respective structural and functional differences between a boy's and a girl's brains, there are also a number of other differences evident when looking at the combination of structure, function and brain chemistry. Table 3.1 offers a detailed overview of numerous other differences identified by medical and scientific research. This table also offers a strong foundation for the remaining sections of this book. This is founded on the belief that understanding some of the differences that exist between the brains of boys and girls facilitates a greater understanding of how various environments, experiences and expectations also impact on a boy's neural development and vice versa; nature and nurture work in tandem to produce various behaviours. Consequently, Table 3.1 is a useful mechanism for framing further discussions in the remaining chapters.

Table 3.1 The sexually dimorphic brain
Note: 'sexual dimorphism' refers to two different structures that vary as a function of sex.

Prominent structural considerations	Function	Gender differences	Significance
Thalamus	Regulates emotional life and physical safety; processes incoming sensory information from all senses except smell; directly or indirectly involved in almost every regulatory activity in the body.	Processes data faster in females especially at certain times in menstrual cycle.	Greater stress and activity in female thalamus at varying times during menstruation.

Cerebellum	Cerebellum means 'little brain'. The cerebellum contains neurons that are extensively connected to other parts of the brain and spinal cord. This region coordinates smooth, precise movement and balance. It also coordinates thought processes.	Stronger connecting pathways in female brain between brain parts.	Females have superior language and fine motor skills; males are less intuitive as fewer parts of the brain are involved in tasking.
Amygdala	Part of the limbic system involved in emotional processing; the limbic system is generally where emotion is processed.	In males, amygdala is larger and demonstrates a different pattern of neural responsiveness to emotional stimuli as compared to females.	Some research suggests a larger amygdala helps make males more aggressive; this may be due to the fact that the amygdala is rich in testosterone receptor cells.

Hippocampus	A pair of curved structures under the inner surface of the temporal lobes that run along each lateral ventricle of the brain. The hippocampi play a key role in the formation and retrieval of long-term memories stored elsewhere in the brain.	Significant difference in size; proportionally larger in females. Researchers have also found that the hippocampus functions differently in males and females with the number and speed of neuron transmissions higher in females.	Aspects of working memory processed differently in males and females.
Corpus callosum	Primary pathway for communication between the two hemispheres of the brain.	Proportionally larger in females with greater synaptic density.	Females able to coordinate the two sides of the brain better and use the entire cerebrum more efficiently. Female superiority at language-based tasks and the processing of emotion partially attributable to this region.

Frontal lobes	Encompassing 41 per cent of the cerebral cortex, the frontal lobes are the CEO of the brain. The prefrontal cortex is directly interconnected to every distinct functional region of the brain.	This region develops and matures earlier in females and is generally more active. Recent research has identified that these regions are functionally different in males and females.	Verbal communication skills are significantly improved in females, as is the likelihood of girls being able to reflect and make responsible decisions at an earlier age.
Pituitary gland	Secretes hormones influencing growth, metabolism, and the activity of other glands. The pituitary gland activates the adrenal gland in response to stress or fear.	Likely more strongly relates to fight-or-flight data from hypothalamus to endocrine gland in males.	Males fight-or-flight response more rapidly engaged.

Hypothalamus	Often called the brain's 'brain', the hypothalamus is an important component in the regulation of emotion. It also regulates body functions in response to internal and external conditions. The hypothalamus is connected to the hippocampus and seems to be involved in everything including thirst, sleep, hormonal secretion, heartbeat, breathing and temperature; also controls arousal.	Female and male cell structures and patterns significantly different; denser in males.	Males possess a greater and more constant sex drive.
Neuro-transmitters	Neurotransmitters are the chemical messengers of the brain. They facilitate or inhibit impulses at the synaptic level of brain functioning Commonly known neurotransmitters include serotonin and dopamine.	Prevalence and availability of certain neurotransmitters varies in males and females.	Differences in how each gender processes sensory stimulation and regulates mood.

Estrogen	Generally described as the female sex hormone. Helps shape gendered neural architecture of brain in utero.	Much more functionally present in females.	In females, estrogen lowers aggression, competition and self-reliance. Also promotes brain cells to be more active when levels are high, allowing the brain to be more alert and absorb a greater amount of information.
Testosterone	Male sex hormone. Principal factor in shaping sex differences in brain organisation.	Much more functionally present in males.	Range of influences, most notably that of exacerbating aggression when levels are high.

Oxytocin	Hormone secreted by the pituitary gland. Promotes bonding and attachment.	Much more functionally present in females. Testosterone in males blocks the effects of oxytocin while estrogen enhances the effects of this hormone.	Assists in childbirth and lactation for breastfeeding and likely strengthens bonds between an infant and mother. Females have greater sensitivity to touch due to the effects of oxytocin and high levels of estrogen. May also be complicit in bonding aspects of relationship building.
Prolactin	Hormone secreted by the pituitary gland. Associated with the production of tears.	Boys and girls have equal amounts until about age twelve when levels plummet in boys as testosterone levels rise.	Males physiologically less able to cry. Grieving patterns and behaviours different between males and females.

Melatonin	Hormone synthesised from serotonin in the pineal gland. Regulates sleep and circadian rhythms and therefore can impact on moods.	At various times females will have higher concentrations of melatonin.	Impacts male and female sleep patterns, especially during adolescence when the onset of sleep, and by association wakefulness, occurs later than it does in children and adults.
Cortisol	Hormone secreted by the adrenal gland during stressful situations. Helps to activate fight-or-flight responses.	Levels will vary between males and females.	Because the male brain is not as efficient at processing emotions, cortisol levels can remain higher in a boy, which in turn can periodically shut down cognitive functions.
Metabolic Rate	Part of the biological process of converting food nutrients to energy.	Male expenditure of energy is 5–10 per cent higher than females. Glucose metabolic activity in regions of the brain varies between males and females.	Males appear to expend greater energy when activating regions of the brain responsible for processing emotions.

Source: Adapted from various works.[76]

Summary

This chapter has focused on sex differences in the brain and the potential implications of such differences in educating and raising boys. In highlighting differences between males and females, there is no suggestion of superiority of one gender over another. Instead, the intent is to provide an overview of how small differences can lead to major challenges for boys when such differences are not recognised or accommodated for by parents and educators. It is also important to note that the existence of the differences presented are based on biology and not something that becomes inculcated via the environment. Indeed, these differences are widely accepted in the neuroscientific and medical community, and as such provide much food for thought in terms of providing the best experiences and environment for educating and raising boys.

4 Working *with* boys physically

It does not take brain science to tell us that boys tend to be in perpetual motion. Whenever they have the chance, they run, chase, and race. They zoom cars, dig in sand piles, and build forts. On their own, you will rarely find them sitting quietly and listening. Boys are naturally wired for movement.[1]

— *Author Ruth Hanford-Morhard*

Before exploring the seemingly boundless energy that contributes to a boy's need for movement and physical activity, it is important to recognise the use of the word '*with*' that permeates this chapter, as well as the next three. The highlighting of the word '*with*' is based on one of the foundational undertones of this book, namely that boys are often penalised for being boys. All too often, parents and educators find themselves struggling with the various aspects of the behaviour of the boys in their lives. Much of this may be due to not truly understanding what goes on inside the heads of those boys. As a result, boys often find themselves in trouble or on the fringes of doing well because the adults around them get frustrated over what is likely a manifestation of the combination of a boy's developmental stage and his gender-specific neurophysiology. In other words, if we are serious about educating and raising boys in a positive fashion, then it should be self-evident that we will need to understand their nature to work *with* them, instead of against them.

Prior to examining the ideas related to working *with* boys physically, it is important to acknowledge that the following pages are not intended to be a prescription for success for all males from birth to adulthood. Nor are the suggestions that are on offer founded on the notion that all boys are the same, or that we must change the boys around us. Instead, the reader is provided with a number of considerations for enhancing the lives of boys based on the belief that what must change is our perception of the vast majority of boys via the types of research and information provided in this book. These ideas are derived from the neuroscientific research available to parents and educators, as well as a number of noteworthy sources who are acknowledged accordingly.[2] The ideas below are also born out of almost four decades of personal experience as an educator and a lifetime of being male.

Before engaging in the ideas and discussions related to working *with* boys, it is also timely to mention that this chapter, and the following three chapters, are not the be-all and end-all when it comes to working *with* boys. In the coming months and years, there are bound to be continuous volumes of work published for improving our interactions with boys. There are also bound to be sceptical and critical opinions of this work, which are welcome as long as they continue to engage in a dialogue for enhancing the life and educational chances of boys. Many times, critique becomes misplaced, and the focus must remain on what will work for boys and how we engage proactively and positively *with* boys. Make no mistake, some of the ideas to follow will challenge the reader to examine their own perceptions, opinions and strategies regarding boyhood, but in the end that is the primary objective. Parents and educators would also do well to scrutinise 'one-size-fits-all' learning environments with this changed understanding of the male brain and how boys learn and interact with others and the world around them. To truly enhance the lives of boys and the lifeworld surrounding boyhood, we must look inwards and dissect our approaches to working with boys. Boys will be, and always have been, boys, so let's begin from that premise and plan accordingly. To this end, and in order to truly devise a plan for working *with* boys, the next few chapters explore the following domains:

- Working *with* boys physically
- Working *with* boys intellectually or academically
- Working *with* boys emotionally or socially
- Working *with* boys spiritually.

Of course, these domains do not operate independently of one another. For example, working *with* boys physically will likely influence how we work *with* boys across other capacities. The separation exists purely to provide the reader with some specific approaches and strategies for each and not to suggest that they operate in isolation with one another. Further to that, we must also remember that as boys mature and grow into men, so too will their ability to compensate for those aspects of their male brain that challenge them when they are younger. The vast majority of boys grow to be fine young men and this needs to be remembered and encouraged.

Finally, while many of the ideas over the next four chapters may resonate with you, some may not. Take what you can and leave the rest. Every reader will find themselves in varying contextual settings, and as such, each is invited to use what is applicable and set the rest aside for another time or opportunity. Furthermore, the ideas presented and related to working *with* boys are not exhaustive or a panacea for ensuring success. Be assured that various individual opportunities will surface regularly and present parents, teachers and students with successful alternatives. In this sense it is crucial for you, the reader, to understand and remember that for all the ideas and strategies on offer, the familial, social and educational contexts of a boy's life require recognition and flexibility, for there will always be boys who need the adults around them to understand who they are and to accommodate for what makes their brains and bodies tick. Perhaps nowhere is this more prevalent than when it comes to understanding the factors that make working *with* boys physically so important.

Movement, physical activity and the brain

We'll begin our endeavour by briefly highlighting the important links between movement, physical activity and the brain for all children and adults. Always keep in mind that although changes to our society and how we work have resulted in humans becoming increasingly sedentary, knowledge of the benefits associated with overall health and physical activity has a long history. For example, school-aged children and adolescents who are physically active are generally physically and mentally healthier: regular physical activity in young people has been associated with reductions in type 2 diabetes, cardiovascular risk factors, sleep problems, depression and anxiety disorders.[3] Concurrently, research across numerous disciplinary fields has continually demonstrated that while movement and physical activity are important for the body and overall health, they are also facilitated by, and important for, the brain. Regular physical activity leads to increases in levels of serotonin, dopamine and norepinephrine which in turn are helpful in alleviating a wide variety of mental health challenges, including stress- and anxiety-related disorders.[4] And while it is beyond the intent of this book to map out all of the mechanisms of the brain that are involved in movement and physical activity, it is important to recognise how physical activity positively impacts on the brains of children and specifically boys.

As explored above, it is now rather axiomatic that physical activity is good for the body. It is worth noting, however, that regular physical activity can also have a positive effect on cognition, memory, brain structure and functioning, and by association learning and achievement.[5] Physical activity also appears to enhance executive functioning in the frontal lobes. If you recall from Chapter 2, the brain's frontal lobes, and in particular the prefrontal cortex, are often referred to as the brain's CEO. Executive functioning refers to many of the higher order thinking activities we engage in on a daily basis and include such things as concentrating, paying attention, reasoning, exerting self-control, emotional regulation, decision-making, problem-solving and many other important components of thinking and cognition. Importantly, there exists a large corpus of research demonstrating that physical activity appears to enhance executive functioning in children and is further enhanced when such activities require 'thinking while doing' or are hands-on learning activities.[6] In other words, physical activity is to be encouraged as much as possible and understood as a priority for the healthy development of all children and particularly boys, who tend to announce themselves physically whenever they can.

A boy's gotta move!

Boys appear to have a boundless source of energy and are in perpetual motion. Movement and physical activity are important for all children, but they appear to be a biological imperative for boys given their physiological and neurological make-up. This is evident even in the earliest stages of a boy's life when their play patterns are far more physical than those of girls. Prior to two years of age, the activity levels of boys and girls show little difference, but somewhere after their second birthday and lasting until at least age ten, and more often later, boys tend to be more active, more aggressive and generally more physical as a result of higher basic metabolism and the influence of testosterone.[7] Nowhere is this more apparent than in a young boy's proclivity for 'playful aggression.'

The importance of play for healthy development has a lengthy history in child development research. Long before researchers could use technology to look at a human brain in action they discovered how playful experiences enhance almost all aspects of child development including, but not limited to, emotional and creative expression, language, cognitive competence, social skills, and physical development.[8] Play is more than an unimportant silly pastime or something to do when all the hard work is done. It is an integral activity for all aspects of child development and 'playful aggression' is one kind of play where boys thrive.

For some, the linking of the terms playful and aggression may seem odd. After all, isn't aggression something that is harmful and bad? The answer to that question is yes, but playful aggression is neither of those things. Playful aggression is a type of cooperative play where all participants enjoyably and voluntarily engage in various types of role-playing that include aggressive make-believe themes, actions and words but where there isn't any intent to either physically or emotionally harm anyone.[9] This type of play can include mock fighting, rough-and-tumble play, superhero play, chasing one another or various other forms of physical behaviour that are never undertaken at the expense of hurting one another. In the main, playful aggression is a form of pretend play that is rare in the play behaviours of girls and is especially significant for boys who tend to announce themselves physically.[10]

At the risk of appearing repetitive, it should not be too surprising that boys are more physical and aggressive than girls in how they play and engage with the world.[11] Being physically active helps to keep a boy's brain active, which is one reason why boys tend to get bored when they are not moving.[12] The need to move is an innate predisposition and evident in the vast majority of boys across cultures, but it is also important to remember that some boys may be less active and physical. This requires parents and teachers to act accordingly by giving boys plenty of opportunity to be active and use their energy positively whenever possible, while at the same time helping them redirect that boundless enthusiasm when needed. Moreover, it is important to remember that movement is a fundamental consideration to the very existence of a healthy brain and as such mobility is a central component to being human. Only creatures that move from place to place require a brain and humans spend the vast majority of their lives moving both physically and psychologically.[13] In this sense, we must remember that boys are not trees and those parents and teachers who continually impose standards on boys that require them to stop fidgeting, sit still, be quiet and confine their learning and experience to one small space would probably prefer working in an orchard rather than in a classroom. *New York Times* bestselling author and family therapist Dr Michael Gurian advocates that all schools incorporate greater opportunities to move, and that the benefits of increasing physical movement include the releasing of pent-up energy, the diminishing of discipline problems and the stimulation of the bored or zoned-out brain.[14] With that in mind, there are a number of key checkpoints that can be made regarding the importance of and strategies for working *with* boys physically.

Checkpoint 1: Wired for action

During all stages of life it is important to recognise and accept the high activity and physical nature of boys and to provide them safe and developmentally appropriate opportunities to engage with the world in a physical manner.

As mentioned earlier, young boys need to engage in rough-and-tumble play and, when doing so, not be labelled as violent or aggressive. Males are naturally aggressive, which may be a by-product of the cerebellum, brain stem and amygdala being more active in males than they are in females; these areas of the brain control physical responses, action and aggressiveness respectively.[15] Testosterone is also a contributor to aggressive behaviours which often manifests into various forms of play behaviour in young boys and competition through childhood, the teenage years and beyond.

For many boys, the type of aggression demonstrable through rough-and-tumble play or some sports is not only fun but also an emotional avenue for releasing tension and developing lasting friendships. Further to that, preventing boys from acting out their aggression in healthy ways or prohibiting activities due to some misguided notion of aggression is likely to increase the chances that the suppressed aggression and physical tendencies of boys will manifest themselves in less healthy and less positive ways.[16] It is better to engage boys in what is natural to them in a proactive and constructive fashion.

Competitive sport also offers many boys further opportunities to engage with the environment in a physical manner. In spite of some calls to eliminate various sports programs due to negative perceptions related to forms of masculinity, competitive sports are highly positive in engaging boys in comradery and emotional development. Boys who do not lean towards sporting activities as areas of interest should be encouraged and supported in other activities incorporating movement, including, but not limited to, dance and drama. Out of school hours clubs (i.e. Scouts) also provide excellent opportunities for boys to develop and nurture their physical attributes and feed their desire to move.

One final aspect of boys' physicality worthy of mention is related to gross and fine motor skills. For boys, gross motor skills continue to develop from birth and become fairly proficient early in life, but coordination and various fine motor skills can be developed in young boys through drawing, beadwork and other activities requiring the fingers to manipulate small objects. Generally speaking, young boys can throw things quite well but will struggle with tying their shoes. This will change over time but in the early years it is beneficial to provide opportunities for boys to work on their fine motor skills whenever possible. The pronounced gross motor skills of boys also has implications for the next checkpoint which focuses on the learning environment.

Checkpoint 2: The importance of place and space

School environments and classroom endeavour must take into account a boy's need to move and the physiological and neurological processes that exacerbate this situation.

In the early stages of life, boys often run into trouble because of their predisposition to fidget and a need to move due to the continued development of their gross motor skills, as noted above. For many boys, this situation becomes increasingly difficult after break times when they move from outdoor activities to classroom endeavour. In these situations, it would be of great benefit to engage boys in activities requiring physical exertion and cooling down prior to formal teaching episodes. Not unlike the structure of an exercise class, high intensity to low intensity exercise for a few minutes can actually help to calm the male cohort of a class and counteract an inability to sit still. Ten minutes of high intensity to low intensity shadow boxing offers one small example of such an activity. Concurrently, it is significant to bear in mind that this type of activity is beneficial for boys of all ages, especially adolescent boys who can often arrive at school tired and listless due to changes in sleep cycles.

Aside from the intermittent activities employed by teachers, schools would do well to begin their days with physical activity. Historically, many schools once did this but as the demands of curriculums grew, the benefits of daily exercise at the commencement of each day diminished into the annals of 'days gone by'. However, beginning the day with 15–30 minutes of light exercise is very beneficial for daily cognitive performance. Numerous studies have demonstrated positive links between exercise and cognition.[17] For example, a study of nearly 200 overweight primary school children found that 40 minutes of daily physical activity over 14 weeks not only improved various aspects of physical health, but also showed improvements in aspects of cognitive performance and maths achievement; just one of many examples of the body–mind connection.[18]

While physical activity is important, and sitting still can present challenges for boys and teachers alike, it is also noteworthy that boys tend to occupy and use greater space when they are learning. Whether they are playing with toys, running around outside or working at tables, boys simply use more space. For younger boys, sitting in groups can be problematic when they are still learning about individual physical space and are often unaware of their intrusion into the space of others. Furthermore, when using tables or desks as shared spaces it is not uncommon for boys to spread their work into the spaces of their female peers. This is often seen as intrusive and misinterpreted by teachers as inappropriate or impolite behaviour.[19] If groups are the preferred option for classroom activity, then it is important for teachers to identify, discuss and elaborate on notions of physicality and spatial awareness and be proactive in determining the needs of each boy rather than assuming all children understand physical space identically and will operate accordingly. Equally important for teachers is an understanding of how movement helps boys focus.

Checkpoint 3: Movement stimulates the mind

Movement helps to break monotony. Boys tend to take longer to pay attention to new stimuli and need greater stimulation to engage the cerebral cortex and as such often appear bored. Movement is a positive facilitator of engaging boys in new learning.

Arguably many generations of teachers were trained in believing that good students stayed 'on task', and being on task meant being quiet, sitting still and paying attention. The traditional belief that paying attention is best served while sitting passively with eyes fixed on a particular individual is one that is not only antiquated but also very detrimental to boys. There is evidence noting that boys react more physically to their learning environment than girls and use their muscles and nervous systems to think and express themselves as well; it may be annoying for teachers, but boys who squirm can learn better than boys who sit still.[20] They may also learn how to sit still by moving!

One of the keys to sitting still and focusing on any task is a frontal lobe function called 'inhibitory control'. Inhibitory control is a key to paying attention and various aspects of self-control. While we are not sure of the biological basis for differences between boys and girls, we do know that this frontal lobe function develops sooner in girls.[21] We also know that movement-based games like 'Simon says', 'red light, green light' and 'duck, duck goose' can help improve inhibitory control.[22] Therefore, these types of competitive activities not only promote physical activity and movement but may also help boys learn how to pay attention when required.

Finally, when they are required to focus, encouraging boys to manipulate objects while listening or being attentive can dramatically increase male responsiveness to classroom endeavour and reduce behavioural problems. Perhaps before they are required to sit or prior to introducing new lesson material, have all students participate in stretching or some form of movement-based activity for no less than five minutes. In fact, new material could be introduced or previous lessons reviewed by incorporating movement as part of the process. In this sense, sitting still is no longer an option. Sitting quietly while squeezing a stress ball, doodling or some other form of movement at a desk is stimulating a boy's brain to learn. Incorporating movement-based activities as part of planning for lessons is just as significant as any other aspect of pedagogy and curriculum and should be a considered an integral component for working *with* boys. So too, should be considerations about what is used to fuel a body in motion.

Checkpoint 4: Feed the brain

A balanced and nutritious diet coupled with appropriate measures to remain hydrated are not only important for physical development but will also impact on behaviour and learning.

One element of healthy development that does not often get enough attention is diet. Diet and nutrition are not only important components of healthy physical development but are also significant factors in brain and neural development and by association cognition, behaviour and learning. Indeed, malnourishment in the early years has been linked to substantial deficits in myelin development, lower IQ scores, slower language development, behavioural problems and sensorimotor deficits and greater neural deficiencies.[23] In other words, one of the best ways to ensure healthy development along with optimal mental and behavioural performance is through good dietary habits.

The causal relationship between nutrition and brain development is very complex but we do know that the brain needs protein and the body needs carbohydrates. The brain must manufacture the right proteins and fats to grow new connections and add myelin to the axons of neurons. It does this via the amino and fatty acids that are ingested to make new proteins and fats. Interestingly, the brain is also an energy hog! It uses somewhere between 20–25 per cent of the energy consumed, depending on age.[24]

The importance of diet and proper nutrition for the developing brain and body cannot be understated. However, the complexities of diet in terms of individual needs is beyond the scope and expertise of this text.[25] Instead, there are a couple of general considerations provided when thinking about what boys should consume. First, if breakfast consists of high simple carbohydrates this will provide a boy with a great deal of energy but it may also exacerbate a predisposition to move. Breakfasts should include foods high in protein and low GI carbohydrates.

Second, water is essential for proper brain functioning and learning. Neurons communicate through electrochemical impulses and the brain communicates with the body though electrical transmissions. Water is essential for all of these electrical processes to occur and given a boy's metabolism and energy levels, water becomes a critical component of keeping the brain alert and ready to learn. Water should always be readily available, especially during warmer times of the year, and not sacrificed for fluids high in sugar and preservatives. Perhaps a good rule of thumb is to consider that often what goes in the body, in terms of simple carbohydrates and sugars, comes out as energy to burn and if there is a desire for concentration and focus in class or studying at home then it would be wise to limit the fuel that can ignite a boyhood fire.

Summary

Perhaps no other aspect of boyhood confounds parents and teachers more than the physicality of boys and their seemingly endless source of energy. On a daily basis, many adults recognise and witness a boy's apparent need for movement, yet attribute desires to move and announce themselves physically as behavioural issues instead of biological imperatives. Movement is not only a necessity for boys but a key component of healthy physical and mental development. Concurrently, the word 'aggression' should not always be viewed as a pejorative; there are ways to be aggressive that are playful and healthy components of development. In the end, failure to recognise, promote and support the various physical aspects of boyhood only sets boys up for failure when their bodies and minds are telling them to move.

Working *with* boys cognitively and academically

Boys and girls do tend to prefer different learning styles ... in many schools insufficient attention is paid to the differing needs of boys and girls and their tendency to favour different learning styles ... a much greater emphasis on raising teachers' awareness of the differences and commonalities in boys and girls preferred learning styles is required.[1]

— *Australian Committee on Education and Training*

The quote above was offered in a special report entitled 'Boys: getting it right', an initiative of the Australian government published in 2002. This report acknowledged differences in how boys and girls approached learning and suggested that the life and educative chances of boys could be improved if parents and educators took into account how boys learn, develop and behave. Adopting part of the framework in that report allows us to look at how we might work *with* boys in terms of developing their academic capacities and enhancing opportunities for success in schools. Equally important, however, is that in identifying strategies in this domain of working *with* boys, we must be sure to take into account that meeting the academic and intellectual needs of boys is not restricted to school entry and age. Long before boys enter schools, pathways to intellectual satisfaction and academic success are forged. To that end, we must first identify how boys learn and how parents and educators might enhance such learning.

One of the most important aspects of healthy brain development, especially in terms of learning and touted in much educational rhetoric, is the need for learning to occur in an enriched environment.

Significantly, the word 'enriched' does not mean to do more but rather to ensure quality of experiences over quantity. In terms of the young minds of boys, this means that we must be attuned to their natural behaviour and how they engage with the environment so that we can ensure they are not missing out on anything.

Infant boys and toddlers begin their learning by actively exploring the environment around them. As discussed in the previous chapter, boys tend to engage with the physical environment with a greater degree of physical play than girls. Males tend to be uniquely interested in 'things', and by association boys like to engage in mechanical and instructional play.[2] Young boys thrive on moving about, putting things together and then pulling them apart. This cannot and should not change, especially in a social climate that is attempting to push academic pursuits onto children early in life. In this sense, the most important thing we can do is ensure that prior to entering the rigour of formalised education, boys are not set up for frustration and failure by being hurried into 'schooling'. This is especially important when we consider that some of the regions of a boy's brain responsible for developing language and verbal proficiency, assets necessary to engage in contemporary educational environments, are developmentally delayed months behind those same regions in girls (Chapter 3 explored some of the disadvantages boys faced in educational contexts due to developmental delays associated with oral language). Therefore, the foremost agenda for working *with* boys cognitively and academically early in their development is allowing them to be the boys they are by simply taking the time to enjoy their often boisterous behaviour, play with them and discuss what is happening in their world to assist in developing their language capacities.[3]

When the time comes for boys to engage in formal education, parents and educators need to be mindful that boys are more vulnerable than girls to academic frustrations. Across almost all aspects of development, boys mature more slowly than girls and are less likely to have mastered the self-control, language and fine motor skills necessary for a successful start in school. However, while boys might have a tougher time than girls sitting still, cooperating and negotiating with their peers, learning their letter sounds and writing in the early stages of schooling, they do have other skills that, when nurtured, can lead to positive outcomes. Following the structure set out in the previous chapter, a broad set of checkpoints for nurturing boys and helping them thrive cognitively is provided below.

Prior to exploring these strategies and ideas it is important to reiterate a few points.

- The brains of boys and girls appear to function differently – particular regions will vary in the duration and operation of cognitive processes, especially with regards to spatial rotation ability, mathematical reasoning, verbal fluency and verbal memory. The male brain appears especially adept at visuospatial ability and tends to do well in most aspects of maths.
- Testosterone plays a significant role in brain development and functioning and influences a boy's language and systemising ability.
- The male brain tends to have a higher arousal threshold, and as such, boys often experience difficulty paying attention to tasks that appear irrelevant or unchallenging.
- The male brain's weak inter-hemispheric connections suggest that boys are often limited in responding to tasks requiring rapid transfer of information from one hemisphere to the next (such as communication).
- Chronologically speaking, boys' brains develop and mature later than girls', and as such, boys may lag behind in educational contexts requiring boys and girls to demonstrate certain proficiencies based on age, especially in the early years (such as standaradised testing like NAPLAN).

Checkpoint 1: Language and literacy

Statistically, boys do not demonstrate the same degree of proficiency in language and literacy as girls (this is visible across all levels of formalised schooling). It is imperative to ensure that boys are not labelled as having a 'learning problem' when in fact they may just be developmentally lagging.

One of the most challenging aspects for parents and teachers working *with* boys cognitively and academically is found when engaging in language and literacy activities. Literacy is a fairly modern convention and loosely refers to a person's ability to read and write. Speaking, on the other hand, has developed over tens of thousands of years, and because it is so instinctive we don't have to teach children how to talk.[5] Reading is a different story, as there isn't a reading centre in the brain, and the neuro-circuitry for both reading and writing has to be developed. Learning to read and write is hard work and literacy does not come naturally to either boys or girls. However, girls have an inherent advantage of acquiring proficiency in most aspects of literacy due to their early development of oral language skills, especially in areas related to phonological awareness and letter recognition; that is the ability to separate, identify and analyse the sounds of language and connect these sounds to letters.[6] By almost all measures, girls outperform boys in all aspects of literacy, so boys require a range of approaches, including phonics and reading opportunities that use the natural-style language of 'real' books that are of interest.[7] In other words, boys appear to do better in all aspects of literacy when direct instruction is supported by approaches and materials that are interesting to boys.

Exactly when to engage in formal literacy teaching is an area of contention. There are many who believe that teaching young children to read and write should happen as soon as children begin school, but there is evidence to suggest otherwise, particularly for boys. Finland, which routinely ranks as one of the most literate countries in the world, does not begin compulsory schooling until children are seven years of age, and only after they enter school do they formally engage in literacy learning.[8] This would suit boys in many respects, given that those areas of the brain that mediate and foster oral language development may take longer to develop than in girls. Substantive systemic changes related to education, however, are often beyond the scope of parents and teachers. Instead we must focus on what can be done to mediate challenges associated with language, literacy and neurodevelopmental delays.

Perhaps the most important initial endeavour can be found in the home learning environment. The first three years of life are crucial for long-term literacy outcomes. The home environment determines the quantity and quality of interactions between children and caregivers. During the first few years of learning, experience-dependent creation of synaptic connections is maximal, and we know that the more words children are exposed to and the more conversations they hear and participate in, the better.[9] Literacy development begins long before a boy enters school and develops as each year progresses. Parents must demonstrate that they value engagement with print media and offer opportunities for boys to do likewise. Given the environment is so significant in shaping a boy's neural architecture, boys should be exposed to books and other print media early in life, and reading should be modelled equally by *significant male* and female figures. It is important for boys to see males reading and to have older males read to them given that many boys believe reading and books are feminine pursuits or something that girls do.[10]

Aside from reading to and with boys, it is also important to encourage boys to articulate what they might be doing, why they are doing it and so on, when they are engaged in various activities. A parent and teacher's ability to question and encourage descriptive language and thought processes is as important as opportunities to open a book or put pen to paper. The spoken word facilitates the development of processes in the brain for engaging in reading and writing. This is why oral language development is such an important precursor to all aspects of literacy and should be encouraged whenever possible.[11] Moreover, both parents and teachers play an important role in supporting a boy's language ability across various developmental periods and therefore may exacerbate the differences between boys and girls by not attending to the needs of boys.

When boys do enter school, it is important for any formal language and literacy teaching to incorporate significant opportunities for boys to focus on activities that are relevant and meaningful to them. Reading materials should contain structures and subject matter of interest to boys.[12] Allowing boys to explore literacy at a pace that suits their ability is particularly important; in the early years of schooling boys will not be reading at the same pace as girls. Frustration and a feeling of failure must be avoided at all costs. In the eyes of a boy, there is nothing more likely to shut down experiences in literacy than appearing inadequate in front of his peers. When a boy struggles and stumbles with some text, it should be apparent that he is attempting to engage at a level he is not ready for and an alternative must be offered. Also, sustained attention on reading aloud can be difficult for all children but may be more problematic for boys: one of the largest sex differences between boys and girls can be found in a boy's inability to sit still, tune out conflicting impulses and focus on the task at hand which makes the demands of reading aloud very arduous for boys.[13] Therefore, small group settings with short opportunities to read aloud are far more beneficial than whole class scenarios stretching over more than ten minutes.

Another factor to keep in mind is that specific cognitive abilities such as auditory capacity, the ability to represent shapes and laterality of focus (a necessary skill for reading from left to right) tends to develop later in boys than girls. This suggests that formal literacy instruction should provide opportunities for separating boys and girls while teaching each accordingly.[14] One final point regarding language and literacy development is that there is a great deal of research available for parents and teachers regarding such development and, in particular, literacy development in boys that goes beyond the context of this work. Literacy development draws on a number of frameworks and theories which in turn necessitates that individuals seek out those resources that fit their home and educational contexts. References for resources that offer sound initial starting points can be found in this chapter's reference list.[15]

Checkpoint 2: Approaches to learning

Learning for boys tends to be most productive when it allows for plenty of 'doing' and elements of competition rather than passively listening and observing.

In Chapter 3, we explored a number of myths related to the brain, gender and learning. It is timely here to mention another myth that permeates many classrooms. This myth is premised on a claim that students have different modes or styles of learning and consequently their learning could be improved by matching teaching with that preferred learning style. And while it is true that children will, if asked, express preferences about how they prefer information being presented to them along with evidence of specific aptitudes for different kinds of thinking and processing information, there isn't any research suggesting that attending to such preferences is beneficial or validates any educational application of learning styles.[16] In other words, there isn't any credible evidence that learning styles exist and any such suggestion that someone is an auditory, visual or kinesthetic learner has no empirical support.[17] However, there are a range of ideas, strategies and theories related to how one engages or approaches learning, and this is an important consideration for working *with* boys. Let's start with how boys generally engage with the world around them.

The previous chapter outlined how important movement and physical activity is for a boy's learning and development. It also described how difficult it can be for boys to sit still for extended periods of time and pay attention to any one thing. Indeed, the activity level of boys is arguably the stuff of legend. Starting between the ages of two and four, boys demonstrate greater activity than girls and this may be due to their higher basic metabolic rate as well as a proclivity to engage in aggressive play and announce themselves physically.[18] Such behaviour is also influenced by various neurotransmitters and hormones that can impact on levels of impatience, irritability, frustration, attention and impulsivity (see Chapter 3 for a review of the details of the interplay of neurotransmitters and hormones on the male brain). In terms of behaviour, boys prefer approaches to learning that are active, requiring classroom endeavours to focus on problem-solving, inquiry and activity as they are more likely to eliminate boredom for boys and stem frustration levels. Giving boys plenty of opportunities to be active will allow them to use their seemingly endless supply of energy positively.[19] Concurrently, learning that occurs outside of the classroom or involves hands-on activities is better placed to meet the needs of boys, as is any opportunity to compete.

One style of educational practice that has been in use for a number of generations is cooperative learning. Cooperative learning has a long history but has become more prominent in schools since the close of the last century.[20] While cooperation is a valuable asset and skill to be learned, it should not diminish the important contribution of competition in a boy's world. Learning environments that offer a degree of competition provide stimulation and engagement to the male brain and help academic performance.[21] The innate desire for competition is evident in studies that found boys will spend 65 per cent of their free time in competitive games while girls will only spend 35 per cent of such time competing; when they do compete, girls take turns 20 times more than boys.[22] Yet while competition is beneficial for most boys, not all boys like to compete and not all competition is positive. Direct competition where individuals compete against one another can be a motivating force for boys but can also be a negative experience that can create behaviour issues. For example, when competition is used by adults or children as a mechanism for comparisons, this can lead to frustration for those who 'lose'. This is particularly true with younger boys who are still learning aspects of what sportsmanship means and how losing can actually be a positive learning experience. Remember that the brain is still maturing, and for young boys, sportsmanship can be an ambiguous concept that takes time to develop. Competition can help in such development. Interestingly, so too can competition that is cooperative.

Cooperative competition involves groups rather than individual competitors. Team sports are a good example of cooperative competition, as are group activities in a classroom. Perhaps the most important factor in using competition positively with boys is the approach taken by parents or teachers. The key is to find a balance between the cooperation and competition while avoiding teaching methods that decry competition altogether. Indeed, the rules often found in competitive activities are also a reminder of the importance of structure for boys and their learning.

Similar to competition, activities that demand excellence, discipline and strict standards offer an approach to learning that is beneficial to boys. Encouraging activities that are hands-on and experiential in nature must be complemented by the focused teaching of skills, concepts and ideas. Some would argue that since the 1980s there has been a move towards progressive education with an emphasis on creativity and self-esteem at the expense of standards.[23] And while it is beyond the scope of this book to look at large systemic and philosophic changes to education and teaching in general, many educational leaders believe today's classrooms fail boys by being too unstructured and even hostile to the structures, standards and spirit of competition that provide many boys with the incentive to learn and excel.[24] Although it was published in 2002, the Australian government's report on boys echoes contemporary concerns around progressivism and recommends that learning approaches for boys include more structured activity, greater emphasis on teacher-directed work, clearly defined objectives and instructions, a return to phonics-based teaching of reading and more male role models.[25] These recommendations for teachers, while significant, must also take into account other key factors related to classroom endeavour and, in particular, how a boy's mind works.

One of the most noticeable differences between males and females, and discussed briefly in Chapter 3, is how the male brain focuses on tasks or pays attention. In practical terms, we know that boys tend to perform better when asked to focus on one task for long periods of time rather than being required to multitask.[26] In itself, multitasking is a common but largely misunderstood term. The brain can actually only ever attend to a single task at a time. Multitasking, therefore, is actually rapid switching from task to task rather than simultaneously doing many tasks. It is the case, however, that we can walk and chew gum at the same time but that is because neither requires our conscious attention. Driving a car and texting, on the other hand, asks the brain to shift attention in ways that are cumbersome, effortful and in this example, often deadly. Moreover, there is evidence to suggest that structural and functional differences in various regions of the brain allow for better multitasking in girls than in boys.[27] In a home and school environment this suggests that parents should limit the number of instructions they give to their sons at any one time. In an educational context, teachers should develop and use learning sequences that allow for the completion of one task, activity or discussion topic before proceeding to another and support this by providing checklists to help facilitate structure and sequential learning. Finally, it is important for teachers at all stages of the educational journey to bear in mind that while positive relationships between teachers and students are important, boys tend to be less concerned with pleasing the teacher than do girls.[28] In terms of approaches to learning this means that boys will be less motivated to study and engage in activities unless they find the material intrinsically interesting and will likely only seek assistance from a teacher as a last resort.[29] Moreover, a boy's innate curiosity typically focuses on understanding how things work by making changes, applying movement, looking at the inner workings of things around them, shifting gears and, where possible, taking things apart. Teachers would do well to facilitate learning experiences that proactively encourage such approaches to learning and not be overly concerned about whether or not boys care about what the teacher thinks. This comparative inattention towards pleasing a teacher is also influenced by the overall learning environment and how a boy makes sense of his class surroundings, which is the subject of the next checkpoint.

Checkpoint 3: The learning environment

Girls tend to take in more sensory data than boys. In a sense, a boy's ability to engage with the learning experiences around him is often compromised by his ability, or inability, to process environmental stimuli.

The human brain takes in a great deal of sensory information every second. We are never ever really aware of all of the information we are absorbing unless we pay conscious attention to it. For example, try this: stop reading, and for the next ten seconds or so listen to all of the sounds you can hear. Chances are that you heard some things you weren't previously aware of while reading until you were primed to listen intently. This is the brain's way of ensuring that we only ever pay attention to the sensory information we are alerted to voluntarily or involuntarily. It is also worth considering that we actually have no idea of how others experience the world and generally assume that we are all hearing, tasting, seeing, smelling and feeling things in the same way. This, however, is not the case and is particularly evident when considering how the senses vary between the sexes.

While there are sex differences across all senses, the two primary means of gathering information about the world are through the eyes and ears. Vision and hearing are important tools both in and out of the classroom, and it turns out that boys maintain some subtle, yet significant, differences in these two processes as compared to girls. For example, on average, girls have greater hearing sensitivity and tend to hear better, while boys are more easily distracted by peripheral noise.[30] This may help explain why boys often have a reputation for being loud and not listening, as they have more trouble hearing higher-pitched sounds and appear more attuned to louder and lower sounds.[31] For parents and teachers this means that you may have to speak more loudly to get a boy's attention and be mindful that most boys like things to be loud.[32] This is not a cue for yelling, but rather a prompt for remembering that soft tones are not likely to get a boy's attention. Don't get angry if a boy continues doing something when you have asked him not to – he simply may not have heard you. This is why instructions for boys may need to be louder and supported by written directions when possible. Boys also respond better to a firm yet respectful tone of voice. Moreover, it is also important to repeat questions and allow more time for boys to respond, especially in co-ed environments.

In terms of visual processing, or seeing, there are also some significant sex differences in how males and females take in and process visual stimulation. One of the best known is that boys are more likely to be colourblind. The visual pathways in the male brain also tend to respond to cooler colours such as blue and green and to things in motion.[33] Remember that boys like to move, and it seems that movement may be biologically wired into the male brain; the ability to localise, track and chase moving objects is as innate to boys as the desire to move, make things move and watch things move.[34] Therefore, activities that work with boys cognitively and academically should allow for sensory-tactile responses and movement. If boys must sit for extended periods of time, provide them with opportunities to fiddle with something (i.e. stress ball), because this not only facilitates some degree of movement but can also act as a calming mechanism. Alternatively, allow for multiple opportunities to disengage from tasks at hand and engage in mental breaks. Stretching, walking around, low intensity movement-based activities and games should be used to reinvigorate the senses and maintain focus. Adults are often afforded opportunities to move and take 'brain breaks' throughout each day serendipitously. Teachers should plan to incorporate structured times to disengage from an activity, shift gears in some manner and then reengage with tasks at hand rather than assume boys can attend for extended periods of time.[35] Such measures are advantageous for boys and girls alike as movement appears to actually reinvigorate the brain and is a constant reminder of the mind–body connection whereby cognition is influenced by our senses and activity in the environment.

Checkpoint 4: Assessing learning

As there should be variation in learning and teaching for boys and girls, so too should there be variation in assessment.

One of the most challenging aspects of any learning environment is determining if, and when, something has been learned. Of course, learning occurs every moment of the day, and not just in school – children arrive at school with a great deal of knowledge and skills each and every day,[36] but this is typically not the learning that teachers need to assess. Learning assessment is an important part of formal education, and the last part of this checkpoint focuses on assessing learning in ways that may be helpful for boys.

First, boys tend to be deductive in their reasoning and thought conceptualisations.[37] Multiple-choice tests and exams requiring short structured answers tend to facilitate this type of reasoning while simultaneously providing a competitive environment that challenges boys. It is significant to note that a proclivity for deductive thinking is not even remotely linked to some notion of superior intelligence or overall cognitive ability. Across most, if not all, aspects of general intelligence and broad cognitive abilities, males and females have equal or nearly equal ability.[38] Variations do occur in specific types of cognitive abilities, but this is not a precursor to any notion of higher intelligence. Instead, a preference for deductive thinking should remind teachers that structuring assessment items to provide for such activity is a helpful tool for uncovering where boys are at in their learning. Teachers have reported that debates, problem-solving, philosophical conundrums and assessment underpinned by principles requiring analytical reasoning also appear to work well with a majority of boys who respond well to assessment designed around time-constrained tasks, competition-induced stress and high-stakes tasks.[39] In other words, the importance of continuous and progressive assessment (formative) that has become very prominent over the last three decades should not override the benefits of competition found in examinations or other forms of summative assessment – a balance is necessary.

And finally, it is worth reiterating that, on average females write, read and speak more words than males. In female groups, girls tend to speak equally often, while in a male group one or two students will often dominate. And while boys may struggle with aspects of literacy as noted earlier, exploring questions and problems that focus on single concepts or those that have a definite finish are advantageous for boys. Conversely, open-ended writing assignments and assessment items requiring elaboration do not favour boys. The already enhanced vocabulary skills of girls due to maturation and neurological structures facilitating language provide an advantage over boys in these types of assessment activities. For boys, writing must be purposeful and relevant and teachers should look to enhance aspects of language through developing specific communication skills rather than relying on creative writing assignments. Having boys engage in the analytical processes involved in deconstructing texts is far more useful and appropriate for boys than writing an imaginative essay.[40] Boys tend to revel in procedural text and assessment looking to ascertain a boy's literate capacities would do well to focus on those types of texts rather than fictitious narratives, which tend to bore most boys. Therefore, like many other aspects of working *with* boys cognitively and academically, some measure of differentiation in how assessment is designed and conducted is an important consideration for determining what boys know and where they need to improve in a scholastic setting.

Summary

The opening quote of this chapter referred to boys and girls having different learning styles. It is important not to confuse this with any myths about preferred learning modalities – we are all visual, auditory and kinesthetic learners whose brains do not emphasise one hemisphere over the other. Instead, and in the context of this work, learning styles focuses on how boys engage with the environment and how they might approach various tasks associated with cognition and learning – the emphasis here is more on behavioural approaches to what is being taught to or asked of boys. Differences between boys and girls in terms of auditory and visual processing, developmental milestones, interests and attention, to name a few, should be part of any decision-making for teaching and learning moments.

Working *with* boys emotionally

Perhaps the least understood area of brain difference is emotive processing ... the female brain processes more emotive stimulants, through more senses, and more completely than does the male. It also verbalizes emotive information quickly. Boys can sometimes take hours to process emotively (and manage the same information as girls). This lesser emotive ability makes males more emotionally fragile than we tend to think.[1]

— Dr Michael Gurian

Quite often, conversations about men's emotions and social skills are fraught with difficulty and contestation, providing much fodder for discussion and debate. Neuroscientists are only beginning to understand the biological basis of emotion and how cognitive functioning uses, interacts and engages with the limbic system. Emotion is messy, complicated, primitive, not easily defined, intertwined with cognition and physiology and as such does not have a single blueprint for successful manoeuvring through its often-stormy conditions.[2] Scientists will continue to unlock mysteries surrounding the brain and emotion, but what is already known suggests that the neurological basis of emotion varies between males and females. This, in turn, affects how boys engage with individuals on an emotional and social level.

Sex differences in the neurological foundations of emotion can often been seen in the day-to-day interactions of males and females. If you recall from Chapters 1 and 3, from the earliest hours of infancy, girls will seek out faces while boys are more interested in objects and things.[3] This early difference, not long after birth and evident across cultures, reminds us that such tendencies are not likely the result of any aspect of socialisation or nurturing. Concurrently, numerous studies have also demonstrated that whether young or old, males are less interested in talking about feelings and personal relationships and females are much better at judging emotional expressions.[4] Such differences in emotional interest, style and processing suggest that well-intentioned ideas about nurturing the emotional lives of boys should always consider biology and the male brain's tendencies for dealing with emotional stimuli in a particular way. Two examples help to substantiate this point.

How the brain engages with emotional stimuli is not fully understood. There is some evidence, however, to suggest that our brains have two important emotional systems called the mirror-neuron system (MNS) and the temporal-parietal junction system (TPJ). The MNS allows us to view emotional stimuli and briefly feel (or mirror) the emotion we see while the TPJ is an analyse-and-fix-it circuit board that searches for solutions to any potential emotional upheaval; MNS is geared for 'emotional empathy' while TJS has been referred to as 'cognitive empathy'.[5] Research suggests that males tend to rely on the TPJ more when processing emotional stimuli, especially from puberty onwards, while females tend to engage the MNS system over the TPJ.[6] This means that faced with the same emotional stimuli, females are more likely to be focusing on the actual emotional foundation of a situation while males focus on how to 'fix' the situation. Readers likely have anecdotal experience of males seeming to bypass the feelings of a situation and instead focus on finding a solution. This often leads to challenges between males and females in terms of finding common ground for any emotionally charged situation. Again, this is not linked to any aspect of socialisation, but is rather an example of different mechanisms of the mind for dealing with emotion across each sex.

A second example of differences in how males and females process emotional stimuli is evident in the interplay of various hormones on the types of circuitry noted above. Testosterone and vasopressin in males affects structures in the limbic system and brain circuitry for processing emotions in ways that are different to the higher levels of estrogen and oxytocin in females. One way scientists have demonstrated these differences is through temporarily increasing levels of oxytocin in males and testosterone in females and then having them participate in various tests of emotional processing. Under such circumstances, men become temporarily more generous and empathetic and better able to infer the emotional state of others while heightened levels of testosterone make females more mentally focused on tasks instead of people.[7] Once again, we can see how innate biological differences can influence emotional processing differently in males and females. These are only two examples of difference, but they are clearly important for considering how to work *with* boys emotionally, and they raise the question of how much impact any degree of socialisation can have on a boy's emotions and emotional processing.

While biology is perhaps the most significant determinant related to working *with* boys emotionally, we cannot negate the important role nurture plays as well. There have been important insights in our understanding of the links between emotion and the cultural and societal expectations of boys. However, one of the worrying trends visible in much of the work related to boys and emotion is the view that boys could be more emotional or display their emotions in ways that are more indicative of how girls process and display their emotional selves. Such approaches tend to perpetuate a deficit model of boys whereby their masculinity is deficient or devoid of opportunities to display emotion.[8] In other words, there is an assumption that the range of emotions often evident in the social interactions and expressions of girls must also be available to boys and it is society that suppresses these through its expectations of masculinity. This notion that the emotional lives of boys are somehow constrained by conventional masculinity is not a scientific hypothesis nor credible in most departments of psychology or neuroscience.[9] There exists a plethora of neuroscientific evidence suggesting that the male and female brain differs significantly in how emotion is processed and expressed.

The impact of social norms and how they may influence emotional behaviour and responses reminds us that it is incumbent upon all who raise and educate boys to understand how a male brain can impact on a boy's emotional status. Daniel Goleman, psychologist and bestselling author of *Emotional intelligence*, acknowledges the emotional differences that exist between men and women. Goleman echoes the studies noted earlier and has suggested that the female brain is actually more sophisticated in terms of its ability to read and express emotion. Importantly, Goleman does not suggest that men become more like women but rather that the spectrum of emotional intelligence needs to account for these differences.[10] Concomitantly, we can no longer simply state that it is nature or nurture that shapes the emotional lives of boys, but rather we must look to see how to work effectively *with* the emotional characteristics of a boy, mediated by his neurological make-up and played out in his responses to the environment around him. The checkpoints below offer some ways of meeting this challenge.

Checkpoint 1: Boys do things differently

Emotions are processed differently in the male and female brain. For example, activity associated with negative emotions is localised in the cerebral cortex of girls and in the amygdala of boys, thus allowing girls to articulate their feelings with greater proficiency.[11]

It is often difficult for boys to express their feelings verbally. This could be linked to how emotions activate both hemispheres of the female brain while emotions only appear to activate the right hemisphere of males.[12] In addition, the larger and denser corpus callosum in females facilitates better communication across the hemispheres, allowing for enhanced verbal dexterity, fluency and articulation of emotion.[13] It is also significant that the *anterior cingulate cortex* and the *orbitofrontal cortex* have been found to be larger in females. Both of these regions play a significant role in emotional processing in social and non-social contexts; their increased size is another example of sex difference in emotional processing.[14] Taken in their entirety, these differences likely contribute to the difficulties males have in expressing emotions as compared to females. Moreover, considering the female brain matures earlier than the male brain, the challenges associated with expressing and discussing feelings extend throughout childhood and the school years. All of this suggests that parents and teachers many need to alter their expectations of the emotional responses available to boys. Expressing emotion through the use of language comes far more easily to girls than boys and timing and patience are important skills. It may take some time before a boy can explain how he feels, if he chooses to do so at all, but there are some things that can be done to help boys along the emotional way.

The first thing to bear in mind is that boys do not read non-verbal communication as well as girls. The male brain is not as effective as the female brain at judging emotional cues via facial expressions, body posture and vocal intonation.[15] In other words, boys require clear articulation of emotional content. Do not rely on boys to pick up nonverbal emotional cues and instead relay any emotional intent verbally whenever possible. And while boys can read anger and aggressive behaviours in other boys very well, they do require clear articulation of emotional intent in other contexts.

Second, when encountering a boy who appears emotionally upset, fragile, stressed or angry, have him draw how he is feeling. Alternatively, provide an opportunity for movement or some form of physical activity. Movement is a great mediator of stress and negative emotion and boys often convert movement into expressing their thoughts and feelings.[16] Engaging in movement-based activity allows a boy the time to de-stress and enhance his ability to articulate his emotional status. Simply walking around and engaging a boy in conversation on anything other than how he feels will assist in facilitating emotionally laden dialogue at a later point in time.

Finally, while boys may struggle with expressing their emotions due to innate characteristics, they can develop their emotional intelligence. Emotional intelligence has been described as an aspect of intelligence dealing with managing one's emotions in association with understanding the emotions of others.[17] Parents and teachers can help boys widen their emotional vocabulary by teaching them about emotions and the labels we use for the many ways we feel. Moreover, modelling any vocabulary associated with emotions whenever possible is a useful mechanism for demonstrating to boys a range of human emotions. Depending on age, most boys likely understand what it means to be happy or scared but may not know the differences between frustrated, angry or enraged.

Checkpoint 2: Understanding boys and stress

Compared to the neurological architecture of a girl, a boy's brain tends to become bored easily and responds to emotionally stressful situations differently.

Stress and fear hinder learning for both boys and girls. The neuroendocrine response to stress does not differ very substantially between males and females – both experience a cascade of hormonal responses produced via the hypothalamus. However, the emotional response to stress generally operates differently in males. For example, males are more likely to engage the fight-or-flight response when stressed, while females adopt a more protectionary response that has been referred to as 'tend-and-befriend'.[18] This is an important consideration for parents and teachers and suggests that different approaches are warranted when engaging with boys who appear stressed. Situations can escalate very quickly with boys when they are stressed and small disagreements can turn into major battles. The fight-or-flight response can be a very primal reaction requiring parents and teachers to remain calm and not become part of any problem. It also suggests that parents and teachers would do well to understand some of the things that can activate a stress response in boys.

One of the most stressful situations for boys occurs when embarrassed or made to feel inadequate, especially in front of peers. It is important for parents and teachers to remember to never use shame to coerce boys into action. Equally important is ensuring that any tasks presented to boys are developmentally appropriate and achievable. Frustration can quickly set in, and a sense of inadequacy develop, when he can't do something that is asked of him. When such circumstances arise, trying to solicit a verbal response or engage in a discussion with a boy who is stressed or who has behaved inappropriately should be done with great diplomacy and patience. Anger and shame will not only shut down learning but will also engage the fight-or-flight response and shut off opportunities to build relationships and articulate problems. In males, a region of the brain for supressing anger, referred to as the septum, is smaller than in females, thereby exacerbating the intensity of any stressful moment and making the expression of anger a more common response for males.[19] This part of the anger-expression circuitry in males is formed in utero, behaviourally reinforced during childhood and hormonally reinforced during the teen years.[20] In the day-to-day reality of working *with* boys emotionally, it is therefore significant to keep in mind that, when angry, boys tend to act out their frustrations given their inability to articulate their emotional thoughts.

Anger is one of our six primary emotions and while a very normal emotion, how it is expressed may require some learning. A first step in assisting boys to express anger healthily is teaching them the language of emotion and the words that accompany anxiety, sadness, depression, shame and embarrassment. Help them build an emotional vocabulary. From there, teach them the how anger feels and what can be done to calm those feelings when they arise.

Another factor that can contribute to a boy's level of stress is boredom. Boredom may seem like the antithesis of stress, but for boys boredom is a form of frustration, and when bored, boys may engage others in less than positive or prosocial ways. Moreover, boys need greater stimulation to engage the cognitive and emotive regions of the brain than girls, and challenge helps to motivate boys. Conversely, environments requiring sustained attention over long periods often frustrate and bore the male brain, resulting in inappropriate behaviour. When apathy or boredom appears, it is better to change the mental state of the environment than single out a boy's behaviour as not fitting in with the task at hand. Alternatively, because the male brain is hardwired for 'systemising', action and problem-solving, boys will generally respond to stress (either their own or others') by searching for a practical solution.[21] As such, empathy is not a powerful arbitrator of emotions in boys. Asking boys how they think someone else might feel is often a failing proposition. Better to ask them how they would feel if they were in that situation or how they might solve the situation at hand. As noted earlier, the male brain appears to be better placed to engage in 'cognitive empathy' and look to fix problems or challenges when able to do so. We should therefore recognise how boys may interact with others, but also provide boys with opportunities to enhance both their emotional and social intelligence.

Checkpoint 3: Enhancing emotional and social intelligence

Testosterone influences emotion. Anger and aggression are exacerbated by elevated levels of testosterone. Testosterone also activates the brain stem and limbic regions associated with survival or fight-or-flight responses. This can also have a corollary effect on social relationships.

Earlier in this chapter, we discussed the work of Daniel Goleman in highlighting the differences between the sexes in terms of our emotional and social development and interactions. Goleman coined the term 'emotional intelligence' in 1995 and followed that phraseology with 'social intelligence' in 2006.[22] And while there are some who might consider Goleman's ideas lacking in empirical rigour, there is no denying his impact on our understanding of the psychology surrounding our emotions and social endeavours. Goleman's work suggests that we can foster emotional and social intelligence through various strategies and structures, which in turn suggests that we can use these same strategies and structures to help boys. Remember that boys may be more easily provoked to anger when frustrated or antagonised, and as such developing social skills and aspects of emotional intelligence should be part of all school curricula across all year levels. In the best interests of both boys and girls, parents and teachers should take opportunities to explore how the brain develops, matures and grows and how this relates to other areas of development in boys. The following ideas provide a minimum of important insights derived from such explorations.

First, testosterone affects a boy's behaviour, particularly in relation to anger and physicality. Boys tend to announce and assert themselves and their emotions physically. Parents and teachers would do well to implement some measure of character education, articulating clearly defined standards, guidelines and expectations. Furthermore, unforeseen problems with anger and frustration in home and school environments can be tempered with ensuring that expectations for behaviour are high and structures for disciplinary procedures are firm and clearly defined. But discipline must be appropriate and not unduly harsh or appear as a tool for embarrassment. Use discipline as a form of guidance not punishment and ensure rewards and praise are immediate and offered at any opportunity.

Second, social relationships with boys tend to be hierarchical in nature and structured by various pecking orders. For sociologists, hierarchies are often cast as inherently toxic as they are based on power relations and the oppression of some for the benefit of a few. This will be explored in greater detail in Chapter 8, but at this stage it is significant to bear in mind that the central framework for this book is presented via our understanding of biology, psychology and neuroscience. In this sense, hierarchies are not simply about power. Hierarchies are critical components of being human and an important aspect of social and emotional development. It is through hierarchies that boys develop an understanding of themselves and others, learn to compete or collaborate and negotiate their place in the world. Some types of hierarchical behaviour appear innate in most mammalian species, including human beings. For example, playful aggression or rough-and-tumble play often occurs in hierarchical structures where there are winners and losers. However, sometimes a winner will need to purposefully lose in order to ensure the occurrence of future playful activity. If such reciprocity does not occur then playful activity will gradually diminish and cease altogether: nobody wants to play with a bully who is only focused on winning at the continual expense of others.[23] In this way, the social benefits of hierarchies are self-evident and foster opportunities for boys to self-reflect and consider their actions.

At any opportunity, boys should be given time to reflect on who they are, how they behave and how they interact with others. This often only occurs as a result of inappropriate behaviour, when in reality it is an important facet of emotional intelligence and needs to be part of a boy's daily repertoire of thinking. Girls will often, and at their own volition, self-reflect through diaries and friends. Structured time for boys to acknowledge their own emotional perspectives and attributes should be a part of their activities at home and school. Such activities do not have to happen in isolation and can be part of various character development programs with one final caveat in mind.

The recommendations above are a few ideas available for parents and teachers, but there is also one final factor worth mentioning here in terms of working *with* boys emotionally. As discussed earlier in this book, the brain goes through a phenomenal process of maturation and neural restructuring during adolescence. Myelin will increase over 100 per cent, thereby providing more expeditious connections between neurons. This growth in myelin will occur in the limbic areas first and faster for girls, particularly in the hippocampus and cingulate gyrus: the areas where emotion, decision-making and intellect often meet.[24] In other words, biological evidence supports the commonly held view that girls display greater emotional maturity sooner in life.

In conjunction with aspects of emotional development during adolescence, risk-taking behaviour tends to become more pronounced, and at times quite dangerous, in boys. Any environmental influences towards increased risk-taking are exacerbated by the level of various neurotransmitters (i.e. dopamine) and changes in neural architecture during adolescence, especially in regions related to the nucleus accumbens and prefrontal lobes. Boys will become involved in greater risk-taking activities as they grow. Their emotional immaturity also plays a role in all of this, and as a result we often find boys involved in highly dangerous situations. To this end, it is imperative that parents and educators not only teach boys about this amazing time in their lives but also look to develop risk-taking activities that operate safely and in a prosocial manner. Competitive sports offer one avenue, but for boys not involved with sport, opportunities to be involved in activities requiring some measure of risk is crucial. Examples of physical activities involving risk may include outdoor education experiences and rock-climbing, while drama and performance-based activities provide avenues for risk-taking of an emotional or psychological nature. To this end, the only real limitation is the imagination of the adults who must take care to ensure that the boys around them do not put themselves in harm's way.

There is a growing body of accessible reference material for teachers and parents detailing how to help boys with their emotional and social development. When planning for working *with* boys in this context, the key for engaging in the emotional lives of boys is not to decry who they are and seek to change them. Rather, as I argue throughout this book, we need to understand boys' underlying neurological differences, and the behaviours that stem from them, and foster environments to accommodate these differences. This is particularly helpful as we move through the next chapter, which focuses on how to work with boys spiritually.

Summary

The human brain is designed to do two things – survive and learn – and to do them in that order. We know that the survival and emotional parts of the brain mature long before the analytical regions can regulate our impulses and desires. The processing of emotions also varies markedly between males and females and as such may make boys more vulnerable to various types of emotional upheaval. For boys and girls, emotional development occurs through social relationships, and for boys this often involves hierarchies and competition. Adolescent boys may display this through risk-taking activities, especially when they are with their peers. This suggests that eliminating or even limiting competition at home or school is not in the best interests of boy,s and fostering prosocial risk-taking activities can help in their development and perhaps keep them from harm's way. Finally, it is imperative to teach boys to understand how emotions can influence behaviour and to provide opportunities for self-reflection.

Working *with* boys spiritually

Spirituality is the relationship of the individual, within the community and tradition, to that which is – or is perceived to be – of ultimate concern, ultimate value and ultimate truth, as appropriated through an informed, sensitive and reflective striving for wisdom.[1]

— *Professor Andrew Wright*

In this chapter we focus on enhancing boys' spiritual lives, ideally through approaches that are informed, sensitive and striving for wisdom. Before we begin, I want to explain two important points. First, one of the underpinning motives for this chapter is the recognition that boys are often penalised for just being boys. This is exacerbated by current social and cultural concerns over the behaviour of some males that is labelled 'toxic masculinity' requiring some measure of social engineering to 'fix' boys lest they themselves become toxic. The undertones of such agendas can be quite pernicious for boys. Investigating various aspects of masculinity is always worthwhile, but we must avoid labelling males as defective, which arguably can crush a boy's spirit.

Second, in using the word 'spirituality', I am not referring to any form of religious doctrine. Of course, religion will play an important role in many boys' lives, but for the purposes of this discussion, we will focus on spirituality, which can be defined as the inner personal nature of one's existence, rather than religion (the beliefs and social practices of groups).[2] There has been increasing interest and a growing body of research looking at a so-called 'spiritual brain.'[3] Many of these studies aim to understand how spirituality impacts the mind, mental health and overall sense of wellbeing. For example, studies linking meditation and spirituality have found that such practices not only enhance the functionality of regions of the brain linked to attention and sensory processing, but also have a positive antidepressant effect due to associated increases in serotonin and dopamine.[4] Scientists have also found that the portion of the brain that processes spiritual experiences is the parietal lobe, or more specifically, the left inferior parietal lobule, and that such experiences extend beyond a person's religiosity.[5] Spirituality, then, given its existential nature, can be variously experienced as a feeling of being connected to nature or embracing a sense of humanity via volunteer work or arguably even something as simple as a sense of elation during a sporting event. Spiritual experiences are personal and can have a profound impact on a person's life, and while much of our brain is very mechanistic in design, much of our consciousness and sense of spirituality is far more subjective and a great deal less predictable.

In this chapter, working *with* boys spiritually focuses on the personal nature of boyhood at the intersection of their behavioural needs and tendencies. An initial examination into some of the esoteric parameters around the term 'spiritual' is followed by an example of how some teachers learned to embrace boyhood. Notions of 'boyhood' are then explored in relation to how tendencies to condemn masculinity are actually antithetical to fostering a boy's sense of self. Unlike the previous three chapters, this chapter does not set out a series of recommendations in the form of checkpoints, given the personal nature of exploring one's spirituality. Educating and raising boys is a value-laden enterprise – homes and schools are not neutral places of teaching and learning but rather settings that shape a boy's identity.[6] Given the importance of identity and the fact that this book has tried to offer informed and sensitive reflections regarding working *with* boys, it seems appropriate to include a chapter on how to do so spiritually.

Searching for the 'spiritual'

Some years ago, I noted a paucity of research linking neuroscience with spirituality.[7] However, research into a spiritual brain has progressed to the point where scientists are identifying the exact locations of the brain related to spirituality.[8] Significantly, it is understood that the brain does much more than passively receive sensory data. It picks out relevant bits of information and engages memory, emotion and language centres as we interpret and respond to the world around us. The brain also selects and amplifies some of the information it processes according to mood and mindset; we respond to the world differently depending on our emotional state.[9] And beyond this level of processing we can also think and reflect on existential questions such as what our purpose might be and how we fit into the bigger picture of human existence. For those who work with boys, these types of questions are not only useful but can also help to foster a positive outlook for all boys.

While we are striving to better understand the boys around us, we must also provide opportunities for boys to explore similar existential questions. The last couple of decades have arguably been increasingly challenging for boys due to negative portrayals of maleness and masculinity. This is exacerbated by limited opportunities in Western societies for boys to engage in existential questions of purpose, explore issues of boyhood, masculinity and growing up male, or participate in activities delineating stages of growth and development. In this sense, we should look to enhance the spiritual lives of boys by providing such opportunities.

While parents are the first, and arguably primary, teachers in a boy's life, schools can provide an excellent context for boys to explore questions of purpose. Historically, most opportunities for boys to engage in discussions of growth and maturation in schools tended to focus on physiological changes occurring in the body during puberty, specifically those changes linked to the reproductive system. Increasingly, schools have provided greater opportunities for boys to look at challenges and issues surrounding relationships, familial make-up and social interactions. These types of topics lend themselves to health, physical education and science curricula across all year levels. However, what is often omitted are opportunities to discuss what is happening with boys neurologically and how this influences who they are and how they might act. The material for this type of learning is now readily available and should be part of any didactic agenda. Understanding what is happening to the brain as we grow and mature is integral to understanding who we are, and is thus a central aspect of working *with* boys spiritually. And while learning about the intricacies of the brain is important, working *with* boys spiritually must also allow for boys to explore the following sorts of questions:

- Who am I?
- Why am I here?
- What does it mean to be male?
- What is masculinity?
- What will happen to me as I grow from boyhood to manhood?

These types of questions are all about one's purpose and meaning in life. Across cultures and history, many of these types of questions were explored through the family or various rites of passage. By contrast, twenty-first century Western society does not do a very good job at imbuing these developmental transitions with spiritual meaning. Teachers, scholars and researchers have recognised that contemporary Western culture is one of the few in history that does not incorporate rites of passage for boys and girls alike.[10] World-renowned anthropologist Margaret Mead believes that the increase in various forms of social pathologies are directly attributable to a decline in sanctioned rites of passage.[11] In other words, the lack of ceremonies or rituals signalling a transition to adulthood may be a precursor to a variety of social problems.

In many respects, the omission of rites of passage is a fundamental issue in how we work *with* boys spiritually. We give boys very little opportunity to participate in activities focusing on who they are and who they are becoming. We also do not provide many opportunities to celebrate transitions and in particular the important transition from being a boy to becoming a man. Attaining legal majority, in terms of the ability to drink alcohol, drive a car, or vote, often becomes the default signal of adulthood, but this kind of 'civic' milestone is not standard across regions and offers little in the way of a meaningful recognition of social and personal transition. This lack of formal rites of passage has meant many boys are learning how to be a man via the media, reality shows and the internet.[12]

Over time and within different cultures, rites of passage have taken on many forms. Many traditional societies had some sort of ritual or initiation for transforming boys into men. Such initiations were rigidly structured, step-by-step forms of inculcating manliness that often involved fear, pain, competition, combat, a symbolism of death and rebirth or a revelation of knowledge by elders or gods.[13] One of last century's pre-eminent interpreters of world religion, the anthropological scholar Mircea Eliade, defined rites of passage as:

> *... a category of rituals that mark the passage of a person through the life cycle, from one stage to another over time, from one role or social position to another, integrating the human and cultural experiences with biological destiny: birth, reproduction and death. These ceremonies make the basic distinction, observed in all groups, between young and old, male and female, living and dead.*[14]

In contemporary Western society there are few, if any, such rituals for boys – the Jewish bar mitzvah perhaps the only exception. Such rituals are also absent for girls. However, traditional and contemporary societies often regard the onset of menstruation as a girl's entry into womanhood – a biological rite of passage with no male equivalent.[15] What is needed, therefore, are opportunities for boys to explore what it means to be male and for those boys entering puberty to experience some form of closure to childhood and a welcoming to manhood. Importantly, such opportunities should be about defining a path forward rather than focusing on past achievements, and schools offer a great context for such work.

Educational institutions can provide a valuable context for exploring transitions and developing such rites of passage. Considering that a boy will spend a good portion of his growing years in a school, it seems logical that *categories of rituals* can be developed to delineate and celebrate various passages of the life of a boy. These can take place in various fashions and involve various participants depending on individual school contexts. Importantly, there is no need to reinvent the wheel, as there are examples of ceremonial functions and activities marking these types of transitions.[16] There are numerous threshold events in the lives of a boy that can act as a starting point.[17] The key is to do a bit of research, find models that may suit an individual context and build programs offering boys the chance to move through life's stages proactively and positively while cherishing all that is good about growing up male.

Searching for role models

One of the most challenging aspects of educating and raising boys in contemporary society is doing so in the absence of adult male role models. There is mounting evidence that growing up male requires growing up with older males, especially fathers.[18] Since the latter part of the last century, many boys have grown up fatherless or without a positive adult male influence and the impact of this is alarming and continues to be of great concern.[19] This is not meant to diminish the roles of mothers or other significant adults in the lives of boys. However, there is a plethora of research indicating that boys who grow up in the absence of significant male figures, especially fathers, are more likely to experience physical or sexual abuse, socio-economic disadvantage, and physical and mental health issues; exhibit behaviour problems at school; receive lower grades or drop out of school; suffer from low self-esteem and motivation; and find themselves in trouble with the law.[20] There is also a substantive body of evidence emphasising the importance of the father during critical neurodevelopmental periods and that the absence of a father can impair many aspects of psychological and mental development and increase the risk of personality disorders.[21] Indeed, the evidence of the harmful effects of father absence could fill many more pages and as such is beyond the scope of this book.[22] Yet while fathers appear to be crucial for healthy male development, they are only one part of an important puzzle for meeting the spiritual needs of boys.

Given the challenges associated with fatherlessness and changes to contemporary nuclear families, many boys may need support beyond a father to help them move from boyhood to manhood. In many societies and cultures studied today and across time, boys also receive attention from the whole community; it is hard to raise a boy without the help of other adults.[23] And while there exist numerous community organisations that can meet the male role model needs of boys, schools are perhaps best placed to do so given the amount of time a boy spends in school. In other words, outside of the home environment, schools provide a fantastic context for nurturing the spiritual needs of boys.

The extent to which schools can meet the spiritual needs of boys is very contextual in nature. Schools associated with specific religious denominations likely offer some facet of spiritual exploration linked with theology, while single sex boys' schools may explore this topic differently, as may co-ed schools. Of course, there isn't any single format for working *with* boys spiritually, which leaves such opportunities open to the imagination of the teaching staff. Perhaps a good place to start, as noted above, would be to develop various rites of passage. They may take many forms, but some examples might include the following.

- Structured opportunities for boys to introduce themselves and discuss what it means to be male or what a 'good man' looks like (such approaches must take into account a student's age and should also be periodically revisited as a journey forward).
- Asking boys to identify a positive male role model and then write to them, explaining how they have been a positive influence by exploring changes they have experienced across a school year.
- Nature-based excursions that require boys to work together (i.e. camping or survival activities), which offer a rich context for spiritual growth and personal development as well as a context for various rites of passage activities.

The examples above are presented as tools for starting a conversation about what can be done in schools to work *with* boys spiritually. Throughout this chapter it has been emphasised that developing such practices requires a high degree of specificity depending on context and the boys at the heart of any such endeavour. It would be fantastic to have a definitive manual on how to achieve positive results on this topic, but that is just not possible given the complex nature of the human brain and the social milieu it must operate in. That being said, it is critical to note that when it comes to facilitating opportunities for boys to explore personal purpose and develop their own sense of spirituality, we must remember that the types of messages we send to boys, day in and day out, will affect how they see themselves in the world.

The mistreatment of boys

> *A five-year-old boy, I learned from reading summaries of various neurological studies … is a beautiful, fierce, testosterone-drenched, cerebrally asymmetrical humanoid carefully engineered to move objects through space, or at the very least, to watch others do so.*[24]

From the initial pages of this book, and interwoven within each chapter, is an underlying desire to ensure that boys are not disadvantaged for simply being boys. The remainder of this chapter will explore this in greater detail by examining how boys may be mistreated due to how they engage with the world as a product of their biology and neurological make-up. And while some might argue that the word 'mistreatment' is perhaps a bit alarmist or hyperbolic, it is purposeful. Boys often find themselves in various forms of strife within the home or school for things that, depending on age and context, may be somewhat out of their control given the neurological and chemical milieu of the male brain. This is not to suggest that there is an overt agenda to harm boys, but rather to remind the reader that penalising boys for things such as impulsivity does not take into account the potential nature of said impulsiveness. Instead, a more nuanced approach to understanding the idiosyncrasies of boys offers a platform for nurturing a 'testosterone-drenched, cerebrally asymmetrical humanoid'.

The early chapters of this book offered some insights for considering nature and nurture as complementary rather than contradictory in terms of the neurological make-up of boys. Indeed, growing volumes of scientific literature identify how the environment around us, and our interactions in that environment, shape our brains.[25] This happens before we ever leave the womb and continues through life with much of the hardwiring of our brain occurring from birth to age three or four and then again through adolescence. This suggests that the treatment of boys, and girls for that matter, has a direct impact on all aspects of their development and neurological function. A negative perception of boys' inherent behaviour can often result in long-term issues, not only for the boys themselves but also those who hold such negative views. Good examples of this are evident when watching how adults engage with or speak of boys.

It is always interesting to see how adults respond to the sight of a group of boys in public, especially adolescent boys. Much of this may be attributable to negative media portrayals, deliberately calculated to provoke outrage and fear. Indeed, the media has a great deal to be accountable for in terms of how it portrays boys. Consider, for example, the tale of two such boys, Corey Worthington Delaney and Hugh Evans.

In January of 2008, at the age of sixteen, Corey Worthington hosted a party in his Melbourne home while his mother and stepfather were on holiday in Queensland. The rebellious teenager arranged the party using social media, despite promising his parents that no party would occur in their absence. Needless to say, the lack of parental supervision coupled with out-of-control numbers and underage drinking resulted in partygoers terrorising the neighbourhood and committing no small amount of carnage. Condemned by many as the actions of a wayward teenage boy, Corey's antics brought him national and international attention via mainstream media.[26] Corey's story was analysed for many weeks and he even appeared for a short time on the television reality show *Big Brother Australia*. The media could not get enough of the teenage boy gone rogue.

Hugh Evans, on the other hand, did not get the kind of global attention that enveloped Corey. Another product of Melbourne's suburbs, in 1995 at the age of twelve, Evans won a World Vision-sponsored contest to visit development programs in the Philippines. This award resulted from his participation in World Vision's 40-hour Famine, a event that raises money and awareness of poverty in developing countries. In 2001, Evans was one of sixteen Australian representatives to participate in The Hague International Model United Nations (THIMUN) held in the Netherlands. In 2003, after helping establish The Oaktree Foundation, an Australian-based non-government organisation, Evans was recognised as the Young Victorian of the Year. The following year, he was named the Young Australian of the Year and also one of ten young people awarded the title of an Outstanding Young Person of the World for humanitarianism or voluntary leadership.

The stories of Corey and Hugh give a stark indication of just what kind of 'teenage boy' mainstream media is interested in depicting. One rebellious boy who garners worldwide fame (or infamy) by making the kind of mistake teenagers are renowned for becomes fodder for folklore and ridicule. Meanwhile another teenager, who is busy changing the world for the better, is not as nearly well-known.[27] It is arguable that this media attention inadvertently elevates the results of bad behaviour. But perhaps this view of boys is in the eye of the beholder.

Aside from the proclivity for focusing on bad news, when it comes to boys, the media will also often take a misguided path of linking violence with masculinity. While it is true that statistically speaking males are more aggressive than females, and the behaviour of boys can often be described as aggressive, there is a big difference between aggression and violence. Linking aggression and violence can paint a picture of masculinity as something negative, and many boys are forced to deal with the emotional baggage that comes with such labels and misconceptions of behaviour. Consider your own reactions to a group of boys in a shopping centre or other public areas. Do you stand clear, and watch out of the corner of your eye for fear of some form of aggression? Much has been written about issues such as these and there has been an increasing trend to equate boyhood with trouble.[28] This begs the question as to what messages might we be sending boys about who they are if we continually see them with such lenses. Moreover, given the interplay between nature and nurture, how might our own perceptions of boys and masculinity be shaping the grey matter of their psyche? These questions are important and should be kept in mind as you move through this exploration of how boys are often misunderstood and penalised due to their nature. To that end, it is pertinent to revisit important aspects of male physicality and energy.

Misreading physicality, impulsivity and energy

Through my career I have had numerous opportunities to present workshops and seminars to parents and teachers. These typically focus on aspects of child development, differences between boys and girls and the links between brain development and behaviour. I have also been asked to engage in various research initiatives in schools at the behest of the principal or school leadership team. One such school-based project some years ago continues to resonate with me, for I have seen similar scenarios in multiple contexts. It also offers a great example of how the behaviour of boys is often misread or misunderstood, resulting in some boys suffering unjust consequences for things they do quite naturally and without malice.

Some years ago I was invited to examine a Queensland primary school's behaviour management program to determine how effective and appropriate it was for delivering quality teaching and learning outcomes. The school had over 700 students and was situated in a lower socio-economic region on the outskirts of Brisbane. The school had a number of classes from preschool to Year 7 and included a special education unit, thereby maintaining a fairly large population of students with a broad range of abilities and attributes. Their behaviour management philosophy was premised on the works of Dr William Glasser (choice theory) and Ed Ford (responsible thinking).[29]

In this particular school the behavioural philosophies of Glasser and Ford were used to underpin a three-step intervention process associated with 'inappropriate' behaviour. When a student was first observed breaking one of six pre-established 'rules', they were asked a series of questions that allowed them to reflect on their behaviour and realise that they had taken the first step towards further intervention. When a second infraction occurred, the student was then removed from his or her peers to an area where further reflection could take place followed by some consultation with the teacher before being re-admitted into the activities at hand; such areas were referred to as 'thinking stations'. If a teacher intervened a third time for 'inappropriate' behaviour then the student was reminded that they 'had chosen to leave', and they were sent to the student support classroom (SSC) where they would need to reflect on their behaviour again and construct a plan for improvement and re-admittance to the school environment. This plan was undertaken when the student was willing to write a plan and was facilitated and guided by the SSC teacher. Such was the day-to-day routine of behaviour management within this school.

My focus on this school here is in no way intended as a criticism of the school or its teachers. The school and its staff were deeply dedicated to ensuring that the school had a safe and supportive learning environment for all students. What is interesting, however, is that when looking at the data on behavioural infractions over a period some very intriguing results surfaced.

The school's dedication to supporting all staff and students was evident in the data that was recorded regarding each student's actions leading to their journey to the SSC. Each and every time a student entered the SSC, they did so with a document identifying each inappropriate behaviour that led them to 'choose' to visit the SSC. This database noted the date, time of admission into the SSC, the inappropriate behaviours and the teachers involved in the process. What immediately stood out from the data was that from the beginning of the school year in January to the middle of August when I first had access to the data, there were 2884 referrals to the SSC. Needless to say, the SSC had a number of 'frequent flyers', as they were often referred to. Perhaps of greater interest is the gender split of referrals and the reasons for the referrals. Of the 2884 referrals, 2423 (or 84 per cent) were boys while 461 (or 16 per cent) were girls. Equally interesting was that the vast majority of referrals for boys focused on 'fidgeting', 'movement' or some form of 'aggression'. The type of aggression ranged from the use of profanity to 'rough-and-tumble play' to outright fighting. In itself, fighting accounted for less than two per cent of the aggressive acts noted. With this information in hand I spent some time with the teaching staff with a view to engaging, and perhaps changing, the perceptions of boys held by teachers while implementing proactive strategies for minimising student visits to the SSC.

One of the first areas for discussion with the staff focused on determining and ensuring that the rules of the school were implemented consistently and without bias towards any student. As many educators know, all too often some students find themselves on a perpetual cycle of identification and intervention which results in their behaviour being continually, and arguably overly, scrutinised. After looking at this with a great deal of depth and detail, the teachers then engaged with what contemporary research says about boys and their behaviour especially in terms of fidgeting, movement and aggression. One of the most revealing insights for these teachers was that boys need to move (as we discussed in Chapters 3 and 4).

Having reviewed the research findings and armed with different lenses for contemplating fidgeting, movement and aggression, a number of teachers began to implement strategies they believed might work to the advantage of their students, with a particular focus on boys. For example, early childhood teachers working with students from preschool to Year 3 implemented various exercise-related activities at strategic times throughout the day. Prior to the beginning of the school day and immediately after breaks, these teachers would have students participate in various physical activities in an attempt to proactively counteract physiological factors contributing to restlessness and fidgeting. One of the activities involved shadow boxing exercises from high to low intensity for a period of 10 to 15 minutes. Overall, they found that when the students engaged in movement-based activities prior to and during focused teaching and learning activities, the boys appeared much more settled and content.

A Year 7 teacher took this one step further by deciding to alter the day-to-day routine of her classroom to incorporate greater movement and autonomy. She reconfigured her classroom so that one desk for each student was situated in a U-shaped format in the centre of the class. On the periphery of this new seating structure were a number of other desks set up as single spaces, paired working stations and group tables. The primary directive she presented to her students was that while any person was providing instruction or information and standing in the middle of the 'U', all other students needed to be seated in the desks of the 'U' and attentive to the person presenting. She also stipulated that being attentive did not mean passively listening but rather students could doodle or manipulate various objects (i.e. stress balls) while attending to the speaker. If the 'U' was unoccupied then students could choose to sit wherever they pleased and move as often as they liked. The results of this simple exercise were both interesting and satisfying.

Initially the change to routine was met with a great amount of student experimentation and exuberant movement. Second-guessing herself, the teacher wondered if she had perhaps created a monster because of the chaos of the class. However, once the novelty wore off, the students became more settled in their desires, selective in their movements and respectful of their new-found autonomy. Interestingly, it appeared that the boys in her class tended to move at greater frequency than the girls, but again this became purposeful and seemed to stem behaviour problems. Gradually this teacher found the need to use traditional classroom management techniques diminishing as the students respected everyone's right to be heard while in the 'U' and their right to move as often as they deemed necessary. In the end, the classroom appeared to be not only calmer but a more enjoyable environment for the students and teacher. Like her early childhood counterparts, this teacher noticed a number of significant improvements in the class and her ability to engage students with learning.

In trying to accommodate her male students, she reported to me that the Year 7 classroom environment changed in many ways. Disruptions and behaviour issues diminished, impulsive behaviour appeared to subside and all students relished their autonomy. Over time there was also a marked decrease in the number of referrals of students to the SSC. At the same time, the overall learning environment improved, not only for the boys but also the girls due to the fact that the teacher spent less time managing behaviour and more time working with students. And finally, the teacher expressed that in making some simple changes to her strategies and perceptions the classroom became a happier environment for everyone.

While this might be just one subjective experience, it is significant and relevant in a number of ways. First, the school and teachers had recognised that the large number of boys visiting the SSC indicated that something was lacking in their approach to their male students, and they were prepared to do something about it. When teachers began discussing changes in approaches and saw the improvements in behaviour, many became committed to continued enhancement of the environment and a better understanding of their male students. One relatively new female early childhood teacher went so far to tell me that because she was one of four female siblings and had two daughters of her own, her only experience in working with boys originated in the classroom. She admitted that she was ill-prepared for the energy levels of the boys in her room and had initially struggled with their 'boyish' behaviour. She was one of the teachers that implemented exercise during the day and subsequently found her approaches to be more boy friendly.

Second, the overall experience helps to illustrate that teachers are able to link theory to practice and begin devising strategies for boys with the male brain in mind. This is an important testimony regarding the ability of teachers to literally change their perceptions and practice with immediate results. In this school, the changes that occurred were not overt policies aimed at boys and their masculinity but rather resulted from the recognition that changing how students might be nurtured in their learning could improve the overall educational environment for all students. Parents armed with similar information might learn to recognise and accommodate the nature of their own children's behaviour.

Finally, the opportunity to engage with new research prompted greater curiosity and initiative among the school's staff for understanding what goes on inside the heads of boys and how neuroscience can enhance learning and teaching. Such insights are useful when we see how 'normal' boy behaviour is often condemned as inappropriate or pathologised. In recognising that boys may have different behavioural tendencies and needs, teachers and parents can avoid such deficit views of boyhood and find ways to meet those tendencies and needs.

Save the males!

Schools are often used to gauge a boy's achievement, but it is usually in comparison to girls. In terms of academic success and what constitutes appropriate behaviour, schools also offer a commonly understood environment with familiar expectations and beliefs about conduct. This is due to the fact that in contemporary society it would be rare to find an individual who, in their lifetime, did not attend school. Moreover, because most people have attended school they have a sense of what a classroom is, what is expected in terms of classroom behaviour and what might constitute success. If you couple this with the opening quotes presented in this book's introduction, it would appear that boys are in trouble – both figuratively and literally – and schools may be the best place to fix the problem.

There is a fairly substantive body of evidence supporting the notion that boys experience less success and enjoyment throughout their primary and secondary education. Some years ago, the data to support such a claim showed that boys:

- were significantly more disengaged with schooling and more likely to be at risk of academic underachievement
- exhibited significantly greater externalising behaviour problems such as antisocial behaviour, inattention and restlessness
- constituted between 75 and 85 per cent of those children in the early years who are identified as 'at-risk' of poor achievement in literacy and reading
- reported significantly less positive experiences of schooling in terms of school enjoyment, perceived usefulness of the curriculum and teacher responsiveness
- were more likely to drop out of schooling prematurely
- were subject to more disciplinary actions during schooling.[30]

These issues do not seem to have improved and indeed extend into tertiary education, where significantly more females than males will enter and graduate from universities across most Western countries.[31] This trend is not only worrying but begs the question as to why so many boys find educational contexts problematic. Perhaps the answer lies not in trying to 'fix' boys or their masculinity but instead fix schools to ensure boys are included on their terms. Remember, boyhood is not a disease that needs to be cured.

Involving boys on their terms recognises that they have different interests, temperaments, abilities, capabilities, expectations and worldviews than their female peers. And while it is true that some of these differences can be attributed to environmental factors (nurture), many are biologically primed (nature).[32] Therefore, helping boys thrive at home and in schools requires us to accept what cannot be changed but also nurture what can. For example, a boy is not hardwired to naturally become a gentleman, instead that behaviour has to be taught.[33] Teaching a boy to be a gentleman is one thing but accepting him for his masculine traits is an important precursor for developing such behaviours. So too is ensuring that home and learning environments are boy friendly and do not regard masculinity as something toxic.

Perhaps one of the single most troublesome and damaging phrases boys often come across today is 'toxic masculinity'. The concept of 'toxic masculinity' has a complex and mixed history but seems to have emerged from a men's movement in the 1980s aimed at counteracting the perceived 'feminisation' of boys by wider society.[33] Since that time, toxic masculinity has garnered much attention in various university courses and academic literature but has also spilled into cultural circulation and political discourse. Today, this term is often used as a descriptor for genuinely bad behaviour, usually associated with violence, exclusively committed by males. Unfortunately, it has also been more widely applied to any type of male behaviour with aggressive or competitive tones, through the belief that such behaviour is a gateway to bar fights, domestic violence and school shootings. And while some men do rape, commit violent acts and exhibit inappropriate behaviour, stigmatising masculinity on the basis of bad attitudes and acts perpetuated by some boys and men is simplistic, unfair and wildly unrepresentative of the vast majority of males...remember Hugh Evans! Moreover, labelling masculinity as toxic fails to take into account that there are all-important differences between healthy and aberrational masculinity.[35] Therefore, rather than overtly or purposefully embarrassing boys for the way they are made, we should teach and nourish healthy masculinity and leave terms like 'toxic' masculinity out of any discussion related to raising and educating boys.

Nurturing healthy masculinity

In one sense, much of this book is about nurturing healthy masculinity. To do so, it is important to remember that such a term is highly contextual. Yes, there are plenty of negative examples of masculinity, but we should also appreciate the masculinity that contributes to the building of roads and cities and fixes things. There are opportunities to label masculinity as commendable and worthwhile and such a mindset is as important as any agenda or framework for fostering positive aspects of masculinity. To further promote working with boys spiritually, the end of this chapter summarises some of the most important factors for nurturing healthy masculinity mentioned earlier.

First, it is important to understand impulsivity and embrace the energy levels and proclivity to move displayed by boys. The first year of school, for example, should not be about sitting at a desk focused on literacy and numeracy.[35] Quite simply, such an emphasis is setting many boys up for frustration and failure. In the first formal year of schooling children do not need to be ensconced in any formal teaching. Instead they need to learn through play. This is particularly important for the energy levels of boys. For some parents and teachers, such a claim may appear flippant or untrustworthy. However, and in spite of any political rhetoric or educational performance agenda, we have known for years that when a child moves from prep, foundation or kindergarten to Year 1 they do not need to be literate or numerate. Instead, good oral language skills are the precursor to long-term school success, and this is best fostered through play-based learning.[37]

The need for movement and the physicality of boys combined with a tendency to aggressive behaviours also requires degrees of patience, acceptance and latitude. Aggression is not a precursor to violence, and boys can be taught to understand the difference at a young age by learning through all manner of play to:

- stop whenever another person says to stop
- say stop when something hurts
- understand that stopping or asking to stop does not make you a wimp.[38]

The human brain is a patterning mechanism and operates very well with consistent boundaries and borders. Young boys learn to harness and moderate their aggression with similar consistency in guidelines and rules. Older boys who exhibit physically aggressive behaviours also require close supervision by adults and should be steered into activities and programs that positively harness that aggression; this is why competitive sports are so important for boys. In lieu of sports, however, parents and teachers should look for opportunities for boys to be physical in ways that suit specific needs and go beyond the allure of video games.

The left field reference to video games here is purposeful. Concerns around boys and video games range from the content of games to the sheer volume of time spent gaming. There is plenty of literature regarding the good, the bad and the ugly of video games, but in the context of this chapter the most prominent concern is the sedentary nature of gaming.

Video gaming is popular with boys, but it must be tempered and guided like other activities. There must be balance to ensure that time spent with other people, being active and experiencing the real world is not forsaken for a virtual world. This is particularly important for of socio-emotional development and nurturing healthy masculinity.

Second, it should be very apparent by now that many aspects of schooling do not seem to suit boys. However, boys who struggle with school may try to hide their difficulties with behaviours such as promoting anti-intellectualism or self-handicapping – the practice of protecting your inadequacies by creating a cause for poor performance.[39] Such behaviours have been immortalised by fictional characters such as Bart Simpson, who promotes being a class clown over addressing any difficulties he may have. In this sense, it is important for parents and teachers to always help boys find success in what they do and to stress the importance of trying one's best. This is also another important reason for boys to identify with positive male role models.

Third, and in relation to the provision of role models, it is important for such role models to exist early in the lives of boys and throughout their developmental and formative years. Early childhood contexts and primary schools very often have few, if any, male staff members. In such situations it is imperative for schools to do what they can to bring older males into the classrooms of young boys. This could mean the promotion of parent or family volunteers, or the use of older male students as reading buddies or other types of mentors.

In secondary school contexts there tend to be larger numbers of male staff and they should be encouraged, as much as possible, to act as mentors or coaches through extracurricular activities or specific mentoring programs. The primary school described earlier in the chapter provides yet another good example for such considerations across all sectors of schooling.

One of the outcomes of the research into the behaviour management program of the school discussed earlier was an innovative program aptly called the 'quality time program'. Given the large number of boys who became the focus of problematic behaviour in the school, one male staff member created a program whereby all male staff members were encouraged to give up some of their non-contact time and share that time with those boys who seemed to be in trouble much of the time. Most of the male staff members participated in the program and engaged in such activities on a daily basis by sacrificing anywhere from fifteen minutes to one hour of time depending on their individual schedules. The activities provided varied depending on the interests and needs of the boys in the program, but the results were highly positive with the most notable outcome being that many boys felt better connected to the school and displayed fewer behavioural problems.[40]

Without knowing it, this school was actively involved in nurturing healthy masculinities, and, like a growing number of schools in Australia, it is on a continuous journey linking the art and expertise of teaching with what brain research tells us about boys and learning. Given the changing expectations of schools and those who operate in the school environment, approaches to engaging boys premised on the notion that boys need to be 'driven' to learn and programmed to adapt fails to recognise that maybe, just maybe, boys are okay as they are and what needs adjusting is our perception of who they are and how to best engage them across all areas of development and maturation. One final point to end this chapter, however, is that working with boys spiritually requires parents and teachers alike to embrace boyhood as positive and send this message to the boys constantly. In doing so, we not only help boys along the road to developing a healthy understanding of who they are and what they are becoming, but we also enhance our own understanding of the boys around us.

Summary

The existential and esoteric nature of the word 'spiritual' makes it very difficult to provide an all-encompassing framework for helping boys develop that part of their character, mind and being. Each context is different and so too will be any measures to work *with* a boy spiritually. At the bear minimum, helping boys develop their spiritual selves requires:

- boys at all ages to reflect on what they think it means to be a boy or a man
- the provision of male role models when they may be lacking
- opportunities to experience rites of passage
- opportunities to focus on, and learn aspects of, positive masculinity.

Providing experiences where boys can explore each of the above at home or in school can only benefit all aspects of their development and help to produce fine young men.

Experiences matter!

8

... the wiring between neurons is arguably the single thing that makes the brain special. For it is the wiring that allows the brain to compute and analyze, reason and perceive. The essence of being an intelligent being is the ability to gather information from the world and use that information to sensibly inform action. [1]

— *Professor Gary Marcus*

Experiences matter. The neuroscientific basis for this claim were set out in detail in Chapter 2, but throughout this book the importance of experiences has been woven, both tacitly and overtly, across each chapter. This final chapter, therefore, extends those insights by offering further information on three different, yet interrelated, types of experiences that impact upon boys. The first of these is schooling, and we'll explore some aspects of schooling that may be inadvertently disadvantageous to boys and not so obvious to most adults. This is followed with a look at how technology may be negatively affecting various facets of development and learning. The final section of this chapter extends discussions on masculinity from Chapter 7 by focusing on the importance of attachment and belonging. An underlying theme resonating through each section is the importance of relationships through all facets of boyhood.

The male brain goes to school

I once heard someone say that one of the problems with education is that it has too many problems. Interestingly, I have heard similar comments about boys. What is unfortunate about this type of sentiment is that it fails to recognise the immense potential that exists for doing amazing things with amazing people. Education in itself, and boys themselves, are not the problem. The problem is that after years of trying we still haven't managed to get some things right, resulting in less than effective learning experiences for many boys. A good starting point for change, therefore, begins with educators knowing more about the brain and learning.

It is important for teachers to remember that, neurologically speaking, learning is a physiological process that begins just after conception and lasts a lifetime. Learning also takes place in stages and is impacted by everyday experiences. Therefore, because learning is both intimately connected with the brain and with experience, educators and policymakers would do well to develop their own understanding of the multifaceted nature of the brain and how this plays out at the intersection of boyhood and various learning environments.[2]

For many individuals, scrutinising education often tends to focus on curriculum, assessment and teaching. All too often the learning environment itself gets little attention or is considered of lesser importance. However, we are quickly learning that the actual learning environment and the policies and structures that affect that environment have major implications for how well boys do in schools.

Managing the environment

Traditionally any discussions around managing a learning environment often focused on managing the behaviour in that space or what is more commonly known as 'classroom management'. Discussed throughout this book is the belief that 'managing' boys necessitates understanding them better. Trying to identify a perfect template for classroom management is almost impossible; no two boys are the same, nor are any two classrooms or schools. Instead, a broad understanding of boyhood offers the foundation for developing the most appropriate strategies for each learning context. This part of Chapter 8 therefore focuses on how the physical environment can contribute to getting the best out of boys.

If you were to look back at classrooms over time and today, one of the first things you would notice is the continued design and use of learning spaces (classrooms) that are four-walled areas with desks and chairs. These essentially 'confined spaces' are problematic, especially when considering how the number of students in a class may affect student outcomes, particularly those of boys. Debates about class size, in terms of student numbers and physical space, have a long and contentious history, but many teachers would suggest that smaller numbers provide better quality and a richer environment for pupils. One of the most documented and cited studies examining the impact of student numbers is the Tennessee STAR (Student Teacher Achievement Ratio) Project. The initial project was a four-year longitudinal study with over 7000 students in 79 schools from kindergarten to Year 3. This study found that classes of fewer than 17 students to one teacher were the most effective and contributed to better grades, fewer behaviour problems and better overall results across a range of behavioural and scholastic indicators.[3] Various follow-up reports found that small class numbers were also linked to higher graduation rates and students who were more likely to go on to post-secondary education.[4]

It should not be surprising that class size, both in relation to student numbers and physical space, have an impact on student learning. For boys, such a consideration is extremely important. The attention that can be provided to boys with fewer students in the room is highly positive and desirable. Moreover, and as noted in chapters 4 and 5, it is boys who are often in need of more space and opportunities to move and tend to take up more space when they learn. Given the male proclivity for utilising greater proportions of space, boys are often reprimanded for inappropriate behaviour as they intrude on the space of others. Much of this could change if numbers were fewer or spaces were larger and adequately resourced with teaching and support staff.

Movement is another factor that has not changed all that much in schools. Today's schools still tend to be rather sedentary environments, and an increased reliance on technology is coupled with heavily regulated movement. This too becomes a disadvantage for a boy whose neurological directives and physiological needs tend to be anything but a recipe for sitting still and passively engaging with events around them. We have already examined the importance of movement to a boy's neurological make-up; however, it is significant to re-emphasise that schools and teachers would do well to integrate movement in the planning of learning activities or as a precursor to sustained learning opportunities.

Altering the environment

Other environmental factors that can impact on learning and behaviour include temperature, lighting, noise and acoustics, clutter, air quality, music and aromas. Some of these factors may not appear obvious to many people. Fresh air, some types of music and the incorporation of some scents actually enhance the environments around us, while noise and cluttered or chaotic environments can be very distracting. For boys who have difficulty maintaining attention, noisy and cluttered spaces exacerbate difficulties when focusing on learning tasks.

Lighting is also something that most of us know about from our own personal experiences. What many may not realise is that bright natural light keeps us more alert and can slow or prevent the production of the sleep hormone melatonin, while fluorescent lighting has been shown to influence levels of the stress hormone cortisol.[5] Cortisol is especially significant in terms of male behaviour. Studies have identified links between cortisol levels in boys and conduct disorder, aggression and antisocial behaviour.[6] The key message here is to do away with fluorescent lighting and ensure as much natural lighting as possible.

For all children attending school and the staff who engage with them on a daily basis, the ambient temperature of the classroom can significantly alter behaviour and learning outcomes. The human brain is very sensitive to temperature and cooler conditions generally provide a more relaxed and attentive atmosphere for learning. Educational studies done in the United States have demonstrated declines in reading comprehension and maths skills when the thermometer exceeds 25 degrees Celsius, while neuroscientific research has demonstrated that higher temperatures and humidity can influence various neurotransmitter levels, which in turn can impact behaviour.[7] This is indeed food for thought in a country like Australia, where a great deal of key learning time is disrupted by high temperatures during warmer months, especially in areas where state governments do not send students home until the classroom reaches 40 degrees.

Looking back over the last few paragraphs, one might suggest that much of the critique made about education is as applicable to girls as it is to boys. This author would agree with that statement up to a certain point. While improvements would greatly benefit all students, and in the end that should be the driving force behind any educational reform, much of what exists is of greater disadvantage to boys than girls. The current model of education does appear to be better suited to the female brain, evident in the number of studies, statistics and research suggesting that boys are not doing well in and out of school. Consequently, if we are sincere in improving the educational lives of boys then we should spend some time focusing on structures and practices that meet their specific needs.

Emphasising what matters most to boys in school

While the physical environment is important to learning, the emotional climate is equally important. A sense of belonging, safety and security are not only significant precursors to learning but also to all aspects of emotional development and stability. If a learner's physiological, safety and belongingness needs are not met, then all other factors integral to academic success cannot be attained.[8] Most schools are very good at ensuring that their students are safe and secure. There are times, however, that some students may not feel like they belong, especially when they are struggling with academic expectations or differences.

Boys and girls alike are adept at figuring out who might be in the 'dumb' (remedial) group. And as we have discussed, in the hierarchy of boyhood, appearing inadequate at anything can lead to a range of negative outcomes, including, but not limited to, frustration, anxiety, anger and apathy.[9] Boys do not like to stand out unless it is related to success. For boys, competition, structure and discipline appear to be very important in terms of most aspects of schooling.[10] If you want to turn a boy off school, have him do things he is not developmentally ready for or where he has no autonomy in finding a path forward. Nowhere is this more apparent than in the subject area of literacy.

Chapter 5 outlined a number of difficulties related to boys and literacy, not least of which was the timing of early instruction. With the language areas of the brain in many five-year-old boys exhibiting the same level of development as those in an average three-and-a-half-year-old girl,[11] trying to teach five-year-old boys and girls to read and write alongside one another places boy at a relative disadvantage. In fact, it does appear that at five years of age girls are better able to adapt to most aspects of academic rigour and expectation presented at such a young age.[12] Equally important to remember is that no amount of 'good' teaching can counteract any developmental delay associated with neural maturation, and trying to force reading or writing on boys when they are not equipped to do so is a disaster in the making. This is not to say that all boys are unable to engage in such activities, but most boys cannot, and this should be accounted for in terms of any curriculum or pedagogical initiatives. Failing to do so can impart a negative view of school in the minds of many boys.

Children's opinions of school seem to form very early and negative perceptions in the first year or so of school are often difficult to reverse as children progress through school.[13] It is interesting to note that children in Finland, a country that routinely tops international rankings of student performance and outcomes, do not begin any formal schooling until they are seven years old.[14] In Australia, however, academic pressure does appear to be moving chronologically downward, where younger children are encountering tasks they may not be developmentally ready for. Worryingly, while the pace of education may have accelerated, a boy's brain does not mature any faster than previous generations, which begs the question, what is to be done?

Trying to map out a prescription that will guarantee success for all boys in school is exceedingly difficult if not impossible. Recall that experiences matter, and all boys share some experiences and not others, especially in the early years of life. What works for boys in school, then, is informed parents and teachers: adults who are informed about the developing male brain and the idiosyncrasies associated with it. It's crucial to always consider that there may be underlying neurological reasons for why boys behave and learn the way they do, and that helping boys succeed in school may require different approaches than those offered to girls. In the end, what matters most to boys in schools are the adults around them to mentor, support and guide them each day. And nowhere is this support more necessary than in guiding boys through the all-pervasive impact of technology on boys and the developing brain.

Boys and technology

In the last few decades, technology has changed most aspects of life, education and work. Screen use and online gaming are important areas of attention when it comes to educating and raising boys. Boys engage with screens for both school endeavours and entertainment, and so we'll begin our discussion with the educative value of technology.

The history of various 'technologies' in schools is diverse and lengthy. In terms of computers and screen devices it was arguably during the 1980s that computers started making inroads into homes, businesses and schools. Today, many types of computers or screen devices are deemed necessary for students and for student achievement in a rapidly changing technological world – there is a common belief that if students are not using screens then they will somehow be left behind. However, the merit of such a position, along with the efficacy of computer use in schools, is worthy of some scrutiny.

First, reflect on the fact that most computer devices, including home computers, tablets, iPads and smartphones, are so user-friendly that instruction manuals are either not provided or offer little more than basic start-up and warranty information. Moreover, considering the history of rapid advancement and innovation in all measures of technology, it is important to question the utility of things such as teaching coding to Australian four-year-old children as is currently the case – will this actually be of any use in a decade when they turn fourteen? This is an important question given the levels of financial resourcing and the growing evidence that technology appears to do little in terms of long-term positive academic outcomes as noted below.

In 2015, a fairly damning and yet not well-known report from the OECD categorically stated that:

> *students who use computers very frequently at school do a lot worse in most learning outcomes, even after accounting for social background and student demographics ...*

> *[and]*

> *... the results also show no appreciable improvements in student achievement in reading, mathematics and science in the countries that had invested heavily in ICT for education.*[15]

Indeed, the OECD's report entitled 'Students, computers and learning: making the connection' makes for interesting reading.[16] Overall, the report provides an in-depth analysis of technology usage in OECD countries and, as suggested in the statements above, the results of this analysis do not present a very positive picture. By way of background, the OECD conducts international assessments of student performance in reading, mathematical and scientific literacy every three years. The Programme for International Student Assessment (PISA) tests 15-year-olds across the three domains noted and publishes those findings to assist governments of participating countries in monitoring educational outcomes against a common framework. Since 2003, the PISA findings, as they are colloquially referred to, have identified that Australia has shown a steady decline in all areas tested.[17] Such results generally garner widespread media attention and political scrutiny, as was the case at the end of 2019.[18] Meanwhile, the 2015 report on technology in schools has never received such attention. This is especially concerning given that Australia's use of technology has increased and its internet usage is higher than any other participating OECD country.[19] This is not to say that there is a causal link between computer use and under-achievement, but the rampant adoption of screens for educational purposes should be considered in light of the following comment by Andreas Schleicher, the OECD's Director for Education and Skills when he stated that:

> *put simply, ensuring that every child attains a baseline proficiency in reading and mathematics seems to do more to create equal opportunities in a digital world than can be achieved by expanding or subsidising access to high-tech devices and services.*[20]

It is worth mentioning here that I am not a Luddite or diametrically opposed to computers in schools, but they are not a panacea for learning. Their use should be carefully monitored and their efficacy in furthering academic achievement carefully measured. This is especially significant given the growing number of collective hours students are spending on screen devices. And while there is evidence to suggest that technology can have a positive impact on some aspects of cognition, there exists an equal body of research associated with technology overuse and wellbeing.[21]

Aside from the issues surrounding the efficacy of technology in terms of academic outcomes, there are also challenges around overall screen time usage and the content within such usage. There is much debate about how much time children should spend using screen devices. In 2016 the American Academy of Pediatrics (AAP) suggested that children between birth and two years of age should not actively engage with screens.[22] Guidelines vary depending on the organisation making such suggestions so it is difficult to attain any concise advice. In spite of this, there is a fairly robust body of evidence noting that technology is not able to replicate the interactions boys need early in life for healthy development and that it has little, if any, place in their lives prior to their second birthday.[23] Moreover, research over the last couple of decades suggests that parents and teachers should be extremely vigilant in how devices are used and what is consumed.

In 2006, a study using seven and fourteen-year-old boys found that playing video games engorged the nucleus accumbens (part of the brain's reward centre) while diverting blood away from the prefrontal cortex (the region responsible for analytical reasoning and a range of other higher order thinking processes).[24] In layperson's terms, this study demonstrated that playing video games is like consuming digital cocaine – a euphoric high is experienced while reasoning and thinking is compromised.

A study published in 2019 found that excessive screen use also contributed to underdeveloped social skills,[25] while another study found that screen use by prekindergarten children, and beyond the guidelines recommended by the AAP noted above, was associated with deficiencies in the brain's white matter associated with language and literacy and corresponding cognitive tasks.[26] All of these studies remind us that the developing brain is shaped by experience, and the brain of a young person is far more malleable and 'plastic' than that of an adult and therefore more susceptible to things going wrong.[27] Furthermore, there are also growing concerns related to the types of experiences boys are having with screens and in particular with excessively violent media content.

The potential for various media to increase behavioural aggression has been debated for some time. Today, boys of all ages are often exposed to violence through television and games, and the realistic nature of many contemporary games and virtual environments is worthy of exploration. It is worth noting that gender differences exist in how males and females use technology: boys typically use technology for gaming while girls are more likely to engage technology for social media platforms.[28] Recent studies suggest that these differences result from gender differences in the brain and can be linked to motivation and the brain's reward systems – males actually appear to crave video games over other forms of media.[29] In fact, brain regions implicated in drug addiction studies have been shown to be more highly activated in males after gaming and as such males appear more biologically prone to developing internet gaming disorders.[30]

Aside from any challenges associated with technology and forms of addiction, there is also a growing concern related to violent media, video games and aggression. Experiences matter, and the brain wires up every second of every day in response to experiences, not in an abstract way, but through physical electrochemical connections. These pathways, in turn, can grow stronger through continued exposure and if that exposure is violent in nature there are reasons to be concerned.

It would be inaccurate to suggest that exposure to violent media makes boys violent; to date there is scant evidence to support such an assertion. However, there is a substantive body of research noting that the consumption of violent media can affect the emotional regions of the brain resulting in a desensitisation to violent acts, a potential to promote aggressive attitudes and behaviour, and diminished empathy and prosocial behaviour.[31] At the same time, it is interesting that violence and empathy share some neural circuits in the brain, and violent media may actually numb those empathetic circuits so that the brain fails to respond when violence is actually occurring.[32] Couple this information with the knowledge that as part of their overall emotional and social development, boys develop their beliefs about social norms and acceptable behaviour based on the content of their experiences. Therefore, any activity that promotes violence is likely to be a risk factor for instilling less-than-desirable behaviour in boys.[33] The important message here is that for boys of all ages, parents and teachers would do well to carefully monitor what goes into a boy's mind given the potential it has to affect what comes out. Moreover, a child's overall development and learning occurs best when they actively engage with people and role models, when they explore the world around them and when their social and emotional world is safe, secure and positive.[34] This is just one of many reasons why bonding with boys and fostering positive relationships are perhaps the most important experiences a boy can have.

Relationships matter

Human beings are social creatures and relationships are integral to our sense of being and belonging. For both boys and girls, the need to connect is as important as the need to breathe. And though the nature of boys' relationships, and the ways they seek to connect, can be quite different from girls, relationships and social interactions are deeply embedded into the mental frameworks of both.

Our need to be with other people and form relationships is literally built into our brains. A good example of this is our desire to help others – a fundamental mammalian behaviour that is observable in non-human primates, suggesting it does not require any form of cultural transmission.[35] This innate tendency is part of the brain's survival mechanism and evident in the knowledge that infants rely on the care and help of parents for their very survival. Significantly, this initial caring and helping relationship extends well beyond infancy in humans and is often surrounded by another aspect of relationships and a neurobiological trait – *love.*

Most people tend to associate the word 'love' with the heart. However, love and attachment ignite the reward and motivation region of the brain in the same way that a desire to quench our thirst or relieve the unpleasant feeling of hunger does.[36] In other words, our needs and desires to feel connected with others uses subconscious survival circuits in the brain. These survival circuits are a neurological reminder of the importance of attachment and relationships to development and learning: we are hardwired to connect.[37]

At all stages in life, attachment to others is critical for both boys and girls, and men and women. As noted above, attachment to a loved one during infancy not only is desirable but also helps to shape a 'lasting psychological connectedness between human beings'.[38] Indeed, attachment is regarded as one of the most significant factors for emotional and social development and is the primary source of a child's self-esteem, security, self-control and a range of social skills.[39] And similar to other aspects of emotional development, attachment changes over time as people mature and relationships evolve. Attachment, in the form of relationships and social groupings, is also an integral aspect of learning.

Remember, human beings are social creatures and the brain is actually a social organ. Positive relationships are therefore key to learning; humans, and by association the human brain, have evolved to be linked to and learn from other brains through emotionally significant relationships.[40] Children and adolescents benefit from parents who foster relationships that are firm, warm and accepting of their needs, and those same parental traits have been shown to characterise effective educators.[41] Children learn best in positive relationships with parents, peers and teachers. Significantly, respectful relationships, friendships, and notions of love and intimacy carry some common traits across each sex, however, attaining such things can vary between males and females. For boys, the very nature of building and maintaining relationships can vary markedly from their female counterparts.

Boys and relationships

Boys often develop relationships through shared activities that are fun, have a degree of utility and maintain a high-action orientation.[42] Playing sports or games, working together on a project or any other shared activity are generally positive platforms for boys to develop friendships and enhance relationships. Boys will look to band together to achieve a common purpose, and regularly spend more time in coordinated group activities where they feel comfortable.[43]

In a family context, the activities noted above might also include the care and protection of loved ones, where boys can demonstrate high levels of 'action empathy' (the ability to take action based on seeing things from another's point of view).[44] If you recall from Chapter 6, when faced with emotional stimuli males have a proclivity for 'fixing' and that innate predisposition is also evident in how males build relationships. Importantly, while capacities such as being able to take on another person's perspective improve with age, even young boys will adopt postures of protection with loved ones in psychologically healthy families and communities.[45]

Aside from building relationships through activities and maintaining an innate protective instinct, boys also foster relationships through the use of humour. Male humour is often characterised by friendly banter or good-natured ribbing and acts as a tacit tool for expressing affection.[46] For boys, humour is also an important mechanism for having fun, for creating enjoyable experiences with other boys, for managing conflict and reducing tensions and as a tool for demonstrating they care about others.[47] Research has also shown that humour has therapeutic properties and boys and men use humour as a tool for healing and coping in times of stress and illness.[48] Once again, this is not to say that girls do not use or have a sense of humour, but rather that this trait is enacted differently between boys and girls and with different intent and objectives. For boys, humour is an important tool for bonding and building relationships. It is, arguably, another example of positive masculinity and how boys build relationships and bond with others differently than girls.

Chapters 6 and 7 of this book discussed some specific aspects of relationship building for boys and you can turn back and reflect on the points made within each for clarification and implementation. At the core of those chapters, and indeed underpinning the whole book, is the belief that educating and raising happy and healthy boys into fine young men necessitates an understanding of what makes a boy tick. It also requires parents and educators to carefully consider how boys are viewed and how masculinity is described. We can teach boys that there are many ways to be men with some being more desirable than others, but we should be careful not to condemn masculinity outright. This requires the adoption of a positive masculinity framework that moves away from addressing what might be wrong with boys, or masculinity, to identifying the qualities that empower boys to improve themselves: qualities highlighted throughout this book. We must also avoid any expectation for boys to act more like girls in their behaviour and learning. Instead, we must let boys know that there exist very important biological reasons for why they may do the things they do, and that those reasons are to be valued. Experiences matter, and knowing as much about boyhood as possible is a good step to developing positive experiences with boys and enhancing relationships with them at home and school.

Summary

This chapter set out to emphasise the importance of experiences in the developing brain and to further expand on those experiences that influence the growth and development of boys. We covered three main areas: learning environments, technology and relationships. For learning environments, we examined various aspects of the physical and emotional environment that are often overlooked. We then discussed the efficacy and potential impact of widespread technology use, with a specific look at a growing list of concerns associated with screen time and digital media content. And finally, we extended the discussion of relationships begun in earlier chapters, and stressed again their importance – there is perhaps nothing more important for educating and raising of boys than how they are viewed by others and the relationships that are fostered within a framework of positive masculinity.

Epilogue

From boys to men – more than pink and blue

Most of my professional career has involved researching aspects of child development, behaviour and learning. For almost two decades I have studied the biological and neurological differences between males and females with a particular interest in engaging parents and educators with the newest research available regarding those differences. And while there will always be scrutiny and debate regarding the origins of sex differences, now is an opportune time to go beyond the nature/nurture dichotomy. Every single day medical researchers, neuroscientists, cognitive psychologists and other experts interested in the workings of the brain and mind are finding and documenting evidence noting the existence of innate sex differences and the influence of the environment on neurological development. In the twenty-first century we have well and truly gone beyond 'pink or blue' as defining factors of gender construction and are now able to see structural and functional differences between the male and female brain. Nature and nurture can no longer act as a horse race with one position jockeying over the other for supremacy. As such, we need to tailor experiences to meet the individual needs and unique qualities of all children. We must also be sceptical and cautious of calls for standardisation of any sort, or a one-size-fits-all approach to education. When calls for 'meeting the individual needs of learners' are bantered around educational circles we must be sure not to ignore the individual circumstances that arise out of gendered brain differences.

As neurological research progresses, parents and teachers should keep abreast of new knowledge to help them understand the often hidden nature of boys. Boys, too, should be provided with opportunities to learn about and understand how their brains and minds grow and mature. Education policymakers would do well to embrace the science and develop and deliver courses and curriculum initiatives targeting human growth and development. It is not beyond the capacity of children to learn about how their brains work along with how their bodies function. This is increasingly important during adolescence, when young people often struggle to understand how their bodies and minds are changing, and curriculum on human development typically focuses on reproduction. Teaching boys about what is happening to them neurologically in conjunction with physiological and biological change is an important step in helping boys understand who and what they are. Before this can happen, we must also learn what the latest research is telling us about what is happening with boys.

My own journey in writing and research over the years has allowed me to put this work together and learn even more than before I started the initial paragraph in the introduction. I continue to learn, and to marvel at what I have learned and how it has provided me with a greater understanding of the nature of boys. Examining the neuroscience has also given me a greater understanding of what might be done to help boys work through boyhood to become fine young men. Of course, I am still learning, and I am confident that this book will provide readers with the opportunity to remind me of what I might have missed or suggest other areas for future exploration. I welcome such insights and view them as an opportunity to build a newer framework for understanding and working with boys. As I have argued throughout, it is important for parents and teachers to continually look for strategies for enhancing the lives of boys, rather than trying to change the boys around them. To this end I offer the following quotes as a summary and to provide a reminder of the work ahead. I hope that you will take up the challenge of looking at your own perceptions and developing new ideas for educating and raising boys.

So overpowering is the wave of research that the standard ways of dismissing sex influences (e.g., "They are all small and unreliable", "They are all due to circulating hormones", "They are all due to human culture", and "They don't exist on a molecular level") have been swept away, at least for those cognizant of the research ... sex influences on brain function are ubiquitous, regularly reshaping findings – hence conclusions – at all levels of our field, and powerfully demonstrating how much "sex matters".[1]

— Dr Leonard Sax

... the 1960s and 1970s saw an ideology that dismissed psychological sex differences as either mythical, or if real, non-essential – that is, not a reflection of any deep differences between the sexes per se, but a reflection of different cultural forces acting on the sexes ... the old idea that these might be wholly cultural in origin is nowadays too simplistic.[2]

— Professor Simon Baron-Cohen

Neuroscientists are only now beginning to study what people on the street have assumed all along, that men and women are different. Men and women approach things differently, they have different cognitive styles ... For decades, neuroscientists treated humanity as a homogeneous mass, ignoring the self-evident truth apparent to every man and woman in the street: males and females are different. But we are finding increasingly that one ignores gender differences in cognition at one's own peril.[3]

— Professor Elkhonen Goldberg

The new science of gender-specific medicine is producing an amazing appreciation of how biological sex modifies the way we operate in the world ... we are different, and vastly so, in every system of the body, from the skin that covers us, to the hearts that beat within our chests, to the guts that process the food we eat. Nowhere is this more true than in the brain, the

3-pound organ that houses all that makes us human: our passions, our insights, our appreciation of the created world, our entire intellectual and emotional lives.[4]

— *Dr Marianne Legato*

Neuroscientists are uncovering anatomical, chemical and functional differences between the brains of men and women...these variations occur throughout the brain, in regions involved in language, memory, emotion, vision, hearing and navigation ... researchers are working to determine how these sex-based variations relate to differences in male and female cognition and behavior.[5]

— *Professor Larry Cahill*

Sex differences can exist without one form being better than the other ... While using biological differences to justify sexism is wrong and harmful, ignoring or denying the existence of such differences can also cause harm.[6]

— *Associate Professor Kevin J. Mitchell*

*... in many schools, insufficient attention is paid to the differing needs of boys and girls and their tendency to favour different learning styles ... **the way forward for both boys and girls is to identify their common and separate educational needs and to implement a policy framework with positive strategies to address those needs.***[7]

— *Australian Committee on Education and Training*

Chapter Notes

Introduction: A war on boys?
1. Barzun 1944, p. 170.
2. Gilbert & Gilbert 1998, p. 14.
3. Loane 1995.
4. Browne & Fletcher 1995, p. 2.
5. Hawkes 2001, p. 9.
6. Whitmire 2012, p. 3.
7. Plato 2016, p. 2716.
8. OECD 2015a.
9. Hoff Sommers 2013.
10. See for example Baron-Cohen 2003, Brizendine 2006, 2010, Blum 1997, Cahill 2005, Geary 2010, Koolshijn & Crone 2013, Linden 2018, Mitchell 2018, Moir & Jessel 1998, Nadeau 1996, Panksepp & Biven 2012, Wheelock et al. 2019.
11. See for example Abbot & Ryan 1999, Cozolino 2013, Diamond & Hopson 1999.
12. See for example Diamond & Hopson, 1999, Berninger & Richards 2002, Hardiman 2003. Plasticity refers to the brain's ability to adapt its neural systems and architecture (at a cellular level) to environmental demands. In a sense, the brain actually grows and develops while changing its functions and structures to respond to new challenges. In educational contexts this is very important as this adaptive process is central to what occurs through learning and teaching; greater stimulation offers greater neural development and capabilities.

13. Richardson 1997.
14. Halpern 2000.
15. Biddulph 1995, p.viii.

Chapter 1: Sex and gender

1. Torgrimson & Minson 2005. See also Hoyenga & Hoyenga 1993, Yarhouse 2015, McGuire 2017.
2. Sax 2002, Soh 2020.
3. Sax 2002, 2017.
4. Sax 2017.
5. Savic et al. 2010.
6. Connellan et al. 2000, Geary 2010.
7. Sax 2017.
8. de Beauvoir 2011.
9. McGuire 2017.
10. Yarhouse 2015. It is important to note the expanding terminologies associated with sexual attraction. For example, asexual refers to a person who is sexually attracted to no one while pansexual is now the more common term for a person who is sexually attracted to anyone regardless of biological sex or gender identity.
11. Linden 2018a.
12. Ibid.
13. Minton 1997.
14. Ibid.
15. Panksepp & Biven 2012, Yarhouse 2015.
16. Bilodeau 2005. It is noteworthy that the term 'transgender' appears as fluid as its suppositions and continues to evolve as a social construct.
17. Gooren 2006, Saraswat et al. 2015, Nota et al. 2017.
18. Panksepp 2005, Panksepp & Biven 2012.
19. Panksepp & Biven 2012, American Psychiatric Association 2013.
20. Australian Human Rights Commission 2014.
21. Wilson & Shalley 2018.
22. Collin et al. 2016.
23. The term 'actual' is used here to demarcate the difference between those individuals who are indeed gender dysphoric, and a relatively new phenomenon related to girls and 'Rapid Onset Gender Dysphoria'. That topic is more pertinent to educating and raising girls and is covered in *It's a girl thing* by this author.

Chapter 2: Understanding the developing brain

1. Wang 2018, p. 34.
2. Eagleman 2007, p. 54.
3. Charles Darwin's book, entitled *The expression of emotions in man and animals* and published in 1872, was one of the first to explore emotions by

observing the behaviours of humans and animals and over 100 years later Joseph LeDoux (2002) noted the contemporary difficulties in doing so.

4. LeDoux 2002, p. 202.
5. See Damasio 1994, 2000, LeDoux 1998, 2002, Lane & Nadel 2002, Panksepp 2005.
6. Gopnik et al. 1999, pp. 7–8.
7. Ratey 2001.
8. Ibid.
9. In 1986, Judith Hooper and Dick Teresi made this assertion in their book, *The three-pound universe.* While computers have changed since then, the analogy is still applicable in that the number of computers necessary would still require a phenomenal amount of space ... fewer than a hundred stories of a building perhaps, but not much fewer.
10. Goldberg 2001.
11. LeDoux 1998.
12. Herschkowitz & Herschkowitz, 2004.
13. Geary 2002, 2010, Herschkowitz & Herschkowitz 2004, Panksepp 2005, Mitchell 2018, Wheelock et al. 2019, Soh 2020. See Moir & Jessel, 1998, for a layperson's description of the gendered alignment of brain structure.
14. Ackerman 1992, Herschkowitz & Herschkowitz 2004, Garrett 2009, Nagel 2014.
15. Berninger & Richards 2002, Linden 2018b.
16. Raman 2018.
17. Marcus 2004.
18. Wolfe 2001, p. 17.
19. Diamond & Hopson 1999, Marcus 2004, Geake 2009, Nagel 2012.
20. Ratey 2001, p. 26.
21. Bruer 1999, Giedd et al. 1999, 2006, Nagel 2012.
22. Chugani 1998.
23. Sylwester 2005.
24. Ratey 2001.
25. Benes 1989, Benes et al. 1994.
26. Jean Piaget is perhaps one of the most influential psychologists of the twentieth century, and his theories still form much child development discourse in the disciplines of education and psychology. For concise interpretations of Piaget's work, see Ginsburg & Opper 1988 or Singer & Revensen 1996. Alternatively, Piaget's own work makes for interesting reading (1928, 1953, 1954, 1971).
27. Graber & Brooks-Gunn 1998, Sisk & Foster 2004.
28. Spear 2000a, 2000b, Giedd et al. 2006, Spear 2013, Nagel 2014.
29. Hall 1904.
30. Dahl 2003.
31. Diamond & Hopson 1999, Strauch 2003, Atkins et al. 2012, Spear 2013, Nagel 2014.

32. Giedd 2004, Giedd et al. 1999, 2006, Sisk & Foster 2004.
33. Huttenlochler 1979, Lidow et al. 1991, Bruer 1999, Seeman 1999, Spear 2000a, Andersen 2003.
34. See, for example, Sowell et al. 1999, Goldberg 2001, 2009, Rosso et al. 2004, Blakemore & Choudhury 2006, Whittle et al. 2008, Asato et al. 2010, Atkins et al. 2012.
35. For a detailed look at aspects of the brain's metabolism and energy use, see Chugani 1994, 1996, 1998, Chugani et al. 1987, 1989. For a better understanding of synaptic pruning during adolescence, see Giedd 2004, Giedd et al. 1999, Huttenlocher 1979, Huttenlocher et al. 1982.
36. For detailed descriptions of how the brain matures during adolescence and the possible implications of this process on behaviour, see Giedd 2004, Giedd et al. 1996, 1999.
37. Giedd et al. 1999.
38. Giedd et al. 1999, Herschkowitz & Herschkowitz 2004, Sylwester 2005, Sabatinelli et al. 2007, Purves et al. 2008, Costa et al. 2010, Casey et al. 2011, Spear 2013, Nagel 2014.
39. Giedd et al. 1999, Sylwester 2003, Giedd 2004, Nagel 2014, Blakemore 2018.
40. Giedd et al. 1996, Blum 1997, Strauch 2003, Brizedine 2006, 2010, Lim et al. 2015.

Chapter 3: Sex differences in the brain

1. Moir & Jessel 1998, p. 5.
2. Andreano & Cahill 2009, p. 248.
3. Aranoff & Bell 2004, p. 12.
4. Panksepp 2005, p. 230.
5. Haier & Jung 2008, p. 174.
6. Mitchell 2018, p. 187.
7. The format used here was modelled and adapted from work done by Legato (2005).
8. Legato 2005. See also Hoyenga & Hoyenga 1993, Kimura 1999 2004, Baron-Cohen 2003, Geary 2010.
9. Moir & Jessel 1998, Eliot 2000 2012, Halpern 2000, Herschkowitz & Herschkowitz 2004, Brizendine 2006 2010.
10. Shaywitz et al. 1995, Harasty et al. 1997, Clements et al. 2006, Howard 2006, Burman et al. 2008. See also Ingalhalikar et al. 2014.
11. Gur & Gur 1990, Gur et al. 1995 1999 2002, Legato 2005, Stoet et al. 2013.
12. Pinker 2002.
13. Moir & Moir 1999, Legato 2005, Panksepp 2005, Brizendine 2010, Mitchell 2018.
14. Gur et al. 1991, Benes et al. 1994, Giedd et al. 1999, Eliot 2000 2012, De Bellis et al. 2001, Cahill 2005, Howard 2006.
15. Kimura 1999, Eliot 2000 2012, Halpern 2000, Ratey 2001, Legato 2002, Panksepp 2005, Brizendine 2006, Ingalhalikar et al. 2014.

16. Legato 2002.
17. Halpern 2000.
18. Gurian 2008.
19. Baron-Cohen 2003. The term 'bridge brain' was coined by Gurian et al. 2001.
20. Gurian & Stevens 2011, p. 16.
21. Legato 2002.
22. Moir & Jessel 1998, Baron-Cohen 2003, Herschkowitz & Herschkowitz 2004, Panksepp 2005, Panksepp & Biven 2012.
23. Nadeau 1996, p. 42.
24. Halpern 2000, Legato 2002, Pinker 2002.
25. Gur et al. 1991, Halpern 2000.
26. Sax 2017.
27. Collaer & Hines 1995, Berchtold et al. 2008, Kiraly et al. 2016, Goyal et al. 2019.
28. Halpern 2000.
29. Kimura 1999, Bornstein, Hahn et al. 2004, Bornstein, Cote et al. 2004, Fenson et al. 2007, Erickson et al. 2012, Tenenbaum et al. 2014.
30. See, for example, Erickson et al. 2012.
31. Burman et al. 2008.
32. Harasty et al. 1997, Diamond & Hopson 1999, Eliot 2000 2012, Legato 2005.
33. Eliot 2012.
34. Hanlon 1996.
35. Toga & Thompson 2003, Kong et al. 2018.
36. Ratey 2001.
37. For an in-depth look at the links between brain lateralisation, language and sex difference, see Shaywitz et al. 1995, Kansaku et al. 2000, Kansaku & Kitazawa 2001, Phillips et al. 2001, Geary 2010.
38. For some detailed insights into how the language abilities and capabilities of each sex are orchestrated in the brain, see Shaywitz et al. 1995, Phillips et al. 2001.
39. Panksepp & Biven 2012.
40. Ratey 2001, Baron-Cohen 2003, Dubb et al. 2003, Shin et al. 2005.
41. Kimura 1999, Eliot 2000, Halpern 2000, Ratey 2001, Legato 2002, Geary 2010. For a look at sex differences in grey matter of the left hemisphere and correlations with cognitive performance, see Gur et al. 1999.
42. Geary 2010.
43. Eliot 2000.
44. OECD 2010 2015a.
45. Moir & Moir 1999.
46. See Sylwester 1997 2005, Carlson 2000, The Society for Neuroscience 2002, McEwen & Seeman 2003, Strauch 2003, Gurian 2011, Muller & Jacobs 2010, Meneses & Liy-Salmeron 2012, Nagel 2012 2014.
47. Mann 2013.
48. Hardiman 2003, Arnsten & Shansky 2004.
49. Gurian 2011.

50. Dalley & Rosier 2012.
51. Nagel 2014, see also Chugani et al. 1999, Dahl 2003, Panksepp 2004, Brizendine 2006.
52. Hawkes 2001.
53. Sapolsky 1997, Panksepp 2005, Panksepp & Biven 2012.
54. Eliot 2000.
55. Gurian 2011.
56. Carter 2000, Damasio 2000 2001, Panksepp 2005, Sylwester 2005, Nagel 2012 2014, Sapolsky 2017.
57. Canli et al. 2002, Gur et al. 2002, Wager & Ochsner 2005.
58. Sylwester 2005.
59. Peiper 1925.
60. Herschkowitz & Herschkowitz 2004.
61. Eliot 2000, Herschkowitz & Herschkowitz 2004, Eliot 2000.
62. See, for example, Ruigrok et al. 2014, Gur & Gur 2017, Ritchie et al. 2018.
63. Connellan et al. 2000, Baron-Cohen 2003.
64. Nadeau 1996, Eliot 2000 2012, Gurian 2011.
65. Eliot 2000.
66. Brizendine 2006.
67. Baron-Cohen 2003.
68. See, for example, Whittle et al. 2011, Lungu et al. 2015, Spalek et al. 2015, Saylik et al. 2018, Fischer et al. 2018.
69. Sax 2005, p. 30. See also Schneider et al. 2000, Wager & Ochsner 2005.
70. Halpern 2000, Eliot 2012, Mitchell 2018.
71. Nagy et al. 2001.
72. Halpern 2000.
73. Gur & Gur 1990, Gur et al. 1995 1999, Legato 2005.
74. Legato 2005.
75. Benes 1989, Diamond & Hopson 1999, Legato 2005.
76. Moir & Jessel 1989, Eliot 2000 2012, Halpern 2000, Goldberg 2001, Baron-Cohen 2003, Gurian & Stevens 2005, Panksepp 2005, Sylwester 2005, Gurian 2011.

Chapter 4: Working with boys physically

1. Handford-Morhard 2013, p.32.
2. There have been a number of authors who have contributed to understanding the 'lifeworlds' of boys. It is beyond the scope of this work to identify all of these individuals but those whose work fits in with the foundational premise of this book are paraphrased and their work adapted accordingly.
3. Biddle et al. 2004, Hills et al. 2007, Australian Institute of Health and Welfare 2009.
4. Ratey 2008.
5. Nagel & Scholes 2016. See also Chaddock-Heyman et al. 2014.

6. Coe et al. 2006, Best 2010, Davis et al. 2011, Guiney & Machado 2013, Chaddock-Heyman et al. 2014, Verburgh et al. 2014.
7. Goran et al. 1998, Maccoby 1998, Geary 2010, Eliot 2012, Sapolsky 1997 2017.
8. Burdette & Whitaker 2005, Hewes & McEwan 2006, Nagel 2012.
9. Hart & Tannock 2013.
10. Hart & Nagel 2017 See also Brizendine 2010, Geary 2010.
11. Halpern 2000, Martin & Fabes 2001, Scott & Panksepp 2003, Jarvis 2006, Pellegrini et al. 2007.
12. Hanford-Morhard 2013.
13. Ratey 2001 2008, Sylwester 2003.
14. Gurian 2011.
15. Hanford-Morhard 2013. See also Eliot 2012, Mitchell 2018.
16. Sax 2005.
17. Nagel & Scholes 2016.
18. Davis et al. 2011.
19. Gurian 2011.
20. Brizendine 2010.
21. Eliot 2012.
22. Ibid.
23. Nagel 2012. See also Eliot 2000, Bellisle 2004, Healy 2004, Rosales et al. 2009.
24. Raichle & Gusnard 2002.
25. Two great sources documenting the links between food, water, the brain and learning are Arnot 2001, and Hannaford 2005.

Chapter 5: Working with boys cognitively and academically

1. Committee on Education and Training 2002, pp. xviii-xix.
2. Baron-Cohen 2003, Del Giudice et al. 2012, Mitchell 2018.
3. Hirsch-Pasek et al. 2004.
4. Eliot 2012.
5. Pinker 2007.
6. Chipere 2014, Price-Mohr & Price 2017, Sigmundsson et al. 2017.
7. Eliot 2012, Price-Mohr & Price 2017.
8. Sahlberg 2010.
9. Rodriguez et al. 2009, Kuhl 2010, Harris et al. 2011, Mol & Bus 2011.
10. Scholes 2017 2018.
11. Hirsch-Pasek et al. 2004.
12. There are a number of references regarding books and reading materials for boys that can be found in most book stores or online sellers. One of the best I have found in Australia is *Boys and books* by James Moloney (2000).
13. Eliot 2012.
14. Committee on Education and Training 2002.
15. For a list of recommendations regarding literacy, pedagogy and curriculum, start with the Committee on Education and Training 2002. For a detailed

look at early literacy skills see Eliot 2000, Herschkowitz & Herschkowitz 2004 and Hirsch-Pasek et al. 2004. If you are interested in understanding the neurological intricacies of language and literacy development, see Berninger & Richards 2002, or similar neurological detail related to boys and literacy see Berninger 1998, Berninger & Fuller 1992, Kimura 1999.

16. Pashler et al. 2008.
17. Riener & Willingham 2010.
18. Maccoby 1998, Goran et al. 1998, Halpern 2000.
19. Neall 2002, James 2007, Gurian 2011.
20. Yassin et al. 2018.
21. Gneezy & Rustichini 2004.
22. Stout 2000, Hoff Sommers 2013.
23. Brizendine 2010, see also Lever 1976, McClure 2000, McClure et al. 2004, Berenbaum et al. 2008, Hirsch 2018.
24. Hoff Sommers 2013.
25. Committee on Education and Training 2002, see also Hoff Sommers 2013 and Christodoulou 2014, for further critique of progressive educational practice with relation to boys.
26. Gurian & Stevens 2005.
27. Gur et al. 1999, Baron-Cohen 2003, Gurian 2011, Gur & Gur 2017.
28. Valeski & Stipek 2001, Pomerantz et al. 2002, McFarland et al. 2016.
29. Sax 2017.
30. McFadden 1998, Gurian 2011, Sax 2017.
31. McFadden 1998.
32. Sax 2017.
33. Lutchmaya & Baron-Cohen 2002, Alexander 2003.
34. Brizendine 2010.
35. Many teachers rely on intuition to know when their students need a mental break. Arguably intuition, in itself, is a gender-specific attribute, and as such many boys do not get the breaks they need due to an educational workforce dominated in number by women. All teachers, regardless of gender, would do well to actively plan for what Michael Gurian and Kathy Stevens (2005) refer to as 'brain breaks'.
36. Nagel & Scholes 2016.
37. Gurian & Ballew 2003.
38. Hyde & Linn 2006, Ceci et al. 2009.
39. Gurian & Ballew 2003, Gurian et al. 2009.
40. Gurian & Ballew 2003, Sax 2005.

Chapter 6: Working with boys emotionally
1. Gurian 2011, p. 31.
2. Ratey 2001.
3. Connellan et al. 2000.
4. Hoff Sommers 2013. See also Hall et al. 2000, Gur et al. 2002, Kret & De Gelder 2012, Thompson & Voyer 2014, Wingenbach et al. 2018.

5. Bastiaansen et al. 2009, Shamay-Tsoory et al. 2009.
6. Schulte-Rüther et al. 2008, Cheng et al. 2009, Yuan et al. 2009.
7. Baron-Cohen & Wheelwright 2004, Eme 2007, Domes et al. 2007, Hermans et al. 2008, Barraza & Zak 2009, Zak & Barraza 2013.
8. An example of this type of work can be seen in Pollack (1998). While Pollack's work offers some valuable insights and ideas about working with boys, there are some areas worthy of scrutiny, especially those that equate an inability to express emotion as some form of socially-constructed deficiency.
9. Hoff Sommers 2013.
10. Goleman 1995.
11. Sax 2005.
12. Baron-Cohen 2003, Howard 2006.
13. Howard 2006.
14. Blakemore & Frith 2005.
15. Baron-Cohen 2003, Geary 2002.
16. James 2007, Ratey 2008.
17. Nagel 2019.
18. Taylor et al. 2000.
19. Brizendine 2010, see also Lindenfors et al. 2007.
20. Brizendine 2010.
21. Moir & Jessel 1998, Baron-Cohen 2003.
22. Goleman's 1995 book entitled *Emotional intelligence: Why it can matter more than IQ*, was on *The New York Times* bestseller list for almost two years with more than five million copies in print worldwide in forty languages and used by educators and business leaders alike. *Social intelligence: Beyond IQ, beyond emotional intelligence* (2006) extends Goleman's work on emotional intelligence and offers a detailed synthesis of the latest findings in biology and neuroscience suggesting that we are 'wired to connect' and emphasising the importance of relationships for every aspect of our lives and wellbeing.
23. Panksepp 2005, Panksepp & Biven 2012.
24. Nagel 2014.

Chapter 7: Working with boys spiritually

1. Wright 2000, p. 104.
2. Walsh 1998.
3. See for example Jha et al. 2007, Ives-Deliperi et al. 2011, Urgesi et al. 2010, Miller et al. 2019.
4. Mohandas 2008. See also Manocha 2013 for a user-friendly guide to enhancing wellbeing and performance through meditation.
5. Miller et al. 2019.
6. Walsh 1998, Connell 2000.
7. Nagel 2006.

8. See for example Mohandas 2008, Urgesi et al. 2010, Miller et al. 2019.
9. Pinker 2009.
10. Sax 2017.
11. Grof 1996.
12. Rubinstein 2013.
13. Herdt 1981, Haidt 2012.
14. Eliade as cited in Grof 1996, p.4.
15. Sax 2017.
16. For an extensive exploration of rites of passage, see Carus-Mahdi et al. 1996. Gurian 1997 2002, Grimes 2002, Lee 2004 and Lewis 1997 also offer various complementary and contrasting insights into the moral and spiritual development of boys and rites of passage. There are innumerable volumes available to those who are interested in this field, and it is best for the reader to seek out those works that are most applicable to the context they are in as examples will vary.
17. See Biddulph 2013.
18. Hoff Sommers 2013 See also McCann 2000, Harper & McLanahan 2004, McLanahan et al. 2013.
19. Gennetian 2005, Cooper et al. 2011, Pougnet et al. 2011, McLanahan et al. 2013, Popenoe 2017.
20. Nagel 2006. See also Hemovich & Crano 2009, Australian Institute of Health and Welfare 2010, Vanfossen et al. 2010, Pougnet et al. 2011, Hoff Sommers 2013, McLanahan et al. 2013.
21. Bambico et al. 2015 See also Lamb 2010.
22. A search on the internet or through any number of Australia's government agencies linked to child welfare can provide a vast array of statistics noting a myriad of challenges for raising boys in fatherless environments.
23. Biddulph 1998.
24. Galyan 2001, pp. 51–52.
25. Pascual-Leone et al. 2005, Ansari 2012, Nagel 2012 2014.
26. Johnston 2008.
27. While anecdotal in nature, I have on numerous occasions (likely numbering in the hundreds) asked people during seminars and conferences if they could identify photos of either Corey Worthington or Hugh Evans. To date, nearly every single group I have presented to can pick Corey by his first name in an instant while not a single person has ever identified the 2004 Young Australian of the Year, Hugh Evans.
28. For more detail, see Hoff Sommers 2013.
29. During this time Dr Glasser's (1998) and Ed Ford's (1997) work had been used by a number of schools nationally and internationally as foundations for working with students. It is important to note that the principal tenet behind the writings of these authors is that behaviour is something which cannot be 'managed' or 'controlled' external to a person's needs or desires.
30. Cresswell et al. 2002.

31. Hoff Sommers 2013, OECD 2015b, Peterson 2018.
32. Commission on Children at Risk 2003.
33. Sax 2007.
34. de Boise 2019.
35. Hoff Sommers 2013.
36. Sax 2007.
37. Hirsch-Pasek et al. 2004, Hirsch-Pasek et al. 2009, Nagel 2012, Golinkoff & Hirsch-Pasek 2016, Yue et al. 2018, Rajan et al. 2019.
38. James 2007.
39. Ibid.
40. Nagel 2001 2003.

Chapter 8: Experiences matter!

1. Marcus 2004, pp. 89–90.
2. Caine & Caine 1994 2001, Bransford et al. 2000, Tokuhama-Espinosa 2011.
3. Finn & Achilles 1999, Schanzenback 2006.
4. Mostellar 1995, Achilles et al. 2008.
5. Jensen 2003.
6. Kirrillova 2003, van Bokhoven et al. 2005.
7. Jensen 2003.
8. Nagel & Scholes 2016.
9. Kindlon & Thompson 1999, James 2007, Brizendine 2010. See also Panksepp 2004 and Panksepp & Biven 2012 for more detail about hierarchies and competence in animal interactions.
10. Committee on Education and Training 2002, Hoff Sommers 2013.
11. Sax 2007.
12. Ibid.
13. Valeski & Stipek 2001.
14. Sahlberg 2010.
15. OECD 2015c, p.3.
16. OECD 2015c.
17. OECD 2010, 2014, 2019.
18. See, for example, Baker 2019, Bolton 2019, Urban 2019.
19. OECD 2015c.
20. OECD 2015c, p. 3.
21. Nagel & Scholes 2016. See also Kearney 2007, Kardaras 2016, Twenge 2017, Lissak 2018, Twenge et al. 2018.
22. American Academy of Pediatrics Council on Communications and Media 2016.
23. Herschkowitz & Herschkowitz 2004, Medina 2010, Owen et al. 2010, Aamodt & Wang 2011.
24. Matsuda & Hiraki 2006.
25. Carson et al. 2019.
26. Hutton et al. 2020.

27. Shonkoff & Phillips 2000, Fox et al. 2010, Nagel 2012, Bastian 2018, Lau & Cline 2018.
28. Desai et al. 2010, Kimbrough et al. 2013, Booker et al. 2018, Viner et al. 2019.
29. Dong et al. 2018.
30. Dong et al. 2018, see also Desai et al. 2010, Borgonovi 2016.
31. Nagel 2014, see also Bartholow et al. 2006, Carnagey et al. 2007, Anderson et al. 2010, Strenziok, Kruger, Deshpande et al. 2010, Strenziok, Kruger, Pulaski et al. 2010, Engelhardt et al. 2011, Kalnin et al. 2011, Greitemeyer 2014, Greitemeyer & Mügge 2014, Brockmyer 2015, Lai et al. 2019.
32. Schenck 2011.
33. Huesmann 2007, Bavelier et al. 2010.
34. Nagel 2012.
35. Mason 2018.
36. Brown 2018.
37. Commission on Children at Risk 2003.
38. Bowlby 1969, p. 194.
39. Gurian & Stevens 2005, Nagel & Scholes 2016.
40. Cozolino 2013.
41. Nagel 2012 2014, see also Eliot 2000, Shonkoff & Phillips 2000, Steinberg 2001 2011.
42. Kiselica & Englar-Carlson 2010.
43. Ibid.
44. Kiselica & Englar-Carlson 2010, see also Kiselica et al. 2008.
45. Kiselica et al. 2008.
46. Kiselica & Englar-Carlson 2010.
47. Kiselica 2005.
48. Kiselica & Engar-Carlson 2010, see also Brooks & Goldstein 2001, Chapple & Ziebland 2004, Strean 2009, Savage et al. 2017.

Epilogue: From boys to men

1. Sax 2017, p. 315.
2. Baron-Cohen 2003, p. 10.
3. Goldberg 2001, p. 89–90.
4. Legato 2005, p. xiv.
5. Cahill 2005, p. 42.
6. Mitchell 2018, pp. 214–215.
7. Committee on Education and Training 2002, p. xviii.

Bibliography

Aamodt S & S Wang. (2011). *Welcome to your child's brain: How the mind grows from conception to college.* New York: Bloomsbury.

Abbot, J & T Ryan. (1999). Learning to go with the grain of the brain. *Education Canada,* 39 (1), 8–12.

Achilles, CM, Bain, HP, Bellott, F, Boyd-Zacharias, J, Folger, J, Johnston, J & E Word. (2008). *Tennessee's student achievement ration (STAR) project.* Harvard Dataverse.

Ackerman, S. (1992). *Discovering the brain.* National Academies Press.

Alexander, G. M. (2003). An evolutionary perspective of sex-typed toy preferences: Pink, blue and the brain. *Archives of Sexual Behavior, 32*(1), 7–14.

American Academy of Pediatrics Council on Communications and Media. (2016). Media and young minds. *Pediatrics, 138*(5), Article e20162591. https://doi.org/10.1542/peds.2016-2591

Anderson, C. A., Shibuya, A., Ihori, N., Swing, E. L., Bushman, B. J., Sakamoto, A., Rothstein, H. R., & Saleem, M. (2010). Violent video game effects on aggression, empathy and prosocial behavior in Eastern and Western countries: A meta-analytic review. *Psychological Bulletin, 136*(2), 151–173. https://doi.org/10.1037/a0018251

Andreano, J. M., & Cahill, L. (2009). Sex influences on the neurobiology of learning and memory. *Learning and Memory, 16*(4), 248–266. https://doi.org/10.1101/lm.918309

Ansari, D. (2012). Culture and education: New frontiers in brain plasticity. *Trends in Cognitive Sciences, 16*(2), 93–95. https://doi.org/10.1016/j.tics.2011.11.016

American Psychiatric Association (2013). *Diagnostic and statistical manual of mental disorders* (5th ed.). https://doi.org/10.1176/appi.books.9780890425596

Andersen, S. L. (2003). Trajectories of brain development: Point of vulnerability or window of opportunity? *Neuroscience and Behavioral Reviews, 27*(1–2), 3–18. https://doi.org/10.1016/S0149-7634(03)00005-8

Aranoff, G. & Bell, J. (2004). Endocrinology and growth in children and adolescents. In M. Legato (Ed.), *Principles of Gender-Specific Medicine* (pp.12-24). Academic Press.

Arnot, R. (2001). *The biology of success.* Little, Brown and Company.

Arnsten, A. F. T., & Shansky, R. M. (2004). Adolescence: Vulnerable period for stress-induced prefrontal cortical function? Introduction to Part IV. *Annals of the New York Academy of Sciences, 1021*(1), 143–147. https://doi.org/10.1196/annals.1308.017

Asato, M. R., Terwilliger, R., Woo, J., & Luna, B. (2010). White matter development in adolescence: A DTI study. *Cerebral Cortex, 20*(9), 2122–2131. https://doi.org/10.1093/cercor/bhp282

Atkins, S. A., Bunting, M. F., Bolger, D. J., & Dougherty, M. R. (2012). Training the adolescent brain: Neural plasticity and the acquisition of cognitive abilities. In V. F. Reyna, S. B. Chapman, M. R. Doughherty & J. Confrey (Eds.), *The adolescent brain: Learning, reasoning and decision making,* (pp. 211–241). American Psychological Association.

Australian Human Rights Commission (2014). *Face the facts: Lesbian, gay, bisexual, trans and intersex people.* https://www.humanrights.gov.au/sites/default/files/7_FTF_2014_LGBTI.pdf

Australian Institute of Health and Welfare (2009). *A picture of Australia's children 2009* (Catalogue Number PHE 112). https://www.aihw.gov.au/getmedia/7f635082-69ca-4709-ae0f-52474a744cd1/phe-112-10704.pdf.aspx?inline=true

Australian Institute of Health and Welfare. (2010). *Child Protection Australia 2008–09* (Child Welfare Series 47, Catalogue Number CWS 35). https://www.aihw.gov.au/getmedia/500d6eeb-b5b1-4035-957c-63c389d8fdc7/10859.pdf.aspx?inline=true

Baker, J. (2019, December 3). 'Alarm bells': Australian students record worst result in global tests. *The Sydney Morning Herald.*

Bambico, F. R., Lacoste, B., Hattan, P. R., & Gobbi, G. (2015). Father absence in monogamous California mouse impairs social behavior and modifies dopamine and glutamate synapses in the medial prefrontal cortex. *Cerebral Cortex, 25*(5), 1163–1175. https://doi.org/10.1093/cercor/bht310

Baron-Cohen, S. (2003). *The essential difference: The truth about the male and female brain.* Basic Books.

Baron-Cohen, S., & Wheelwright, S. (2004). The empathy quotient: An investigation of adults with Asperger syndrome or high functioning autism, and normal sex differences. *Journal of Autism and Developmental Disorders, 34*(2), 163–175. https://doi.org/10.1023/B:JADD.0000022607.19833.00

Barraza, J. A., & Zak, P. J. (2009). Empathy towards strangers triggers oxytocin release and subsequent generosity. *Annals of the New York Academy of Sciences, 1167*(1), 182–189. https://doi.org/10.1111/j.1749-6632.2009.04504.x

Bartholow, B., Bushman, B., & Sestir, M. (2006). Chronic violent video game exposure and desensitization to violence: behavioral and event-related brain potential data. *Journal of Experimental Social Psychology, 42*(4), 532–539. https://doi.org/10.1016/j.jesp.2005.08.006

Barzun, J. (1944). *We who teach.* Victor Gollancz.

Bastian, A. (2018). Children's brains are different. In D. J. Linden (Ed.), *Think tank: Forty neuroscientists explore the roots of human experience* (pp. 40-44). Yale University Press.

Bastiaansen, J. A. C. J., Thioux, M., & Keysers, C. (2009). Evidence for mirror systems in emotions. *Philosophical Transactions of the Royal Society B Biological Sciences, 364*(1528), 2391-2404. https://doi.org/10.1098/rstb.2009.0058

Bavelier, D., Green, C. S., & Dye, M. W. G. (2010). Children, wired: For better and for worse. *Neuron, 67*(5), 692-701. https://doi.org/10.1016/j.neuron.2010.08.035

Benes, F. M. (1989). Myelination of cortical-hippocampal relays during late adolescence. *Schizophrenia Bulletin, 15*(4), 585-93.

Benes, F. M., Turtle, M., Khan, Y., & Farol, P. (1994). Myelination of a key relay zone in the hippocampal formation occurs in the human brain during childhood, adolescence and adulthood. *Archives of General Psychiatry, 51*(6), 477-484.

Berchtold, N. C., Cribbs, D. C., Coleman, P. D., Rogers, J., Head, E., Kim, R., Beach, T., Miller, C., Troncoso, J., Trojanowski, J. Q., Zielke, H. R., & Cotman, C. W. (2008). Gene expression changes in the course of normal brain aging are sexually dimorphic. *Proceedings of the National Academy of Sciences, 105*(40), 15605-15610. https://doi.org/10.1073/pnas.0806883105

Berenbaum, S. A., Martin, C. L., Hanish, L. D., Briggs, P. T., & Fabes, R. A. (2008). Sex differences in children's play. In J. B. Becker, K. Berkley, N. Geary, E. Hampson, J. P. Herman & E. A. Young (Eds.), *Sex differences in the brain: From genes to behavior,* (pp. 275-290). Oxford University Press.

Berninger, V. W. (1998). *Process assessment of the learner: Guides for reading and writing intervention.* The Psychological Corporation.

Berninger, V. W., & Fuller, F. (1992). Gender differences in orthographic, verbal and compositional fluency: Implications for diagnosis of writing disabilities in primary grade children. *Journal of School Psychology, 30*(4), 363-382.

Berninger, V. W., & Richards, T. L. (2002). *Brain literacy for educators and psychologists.* Elsevier.

Bellisle, F. (2004). Effects of diet on behaviour and cognition in children. *British Journal of Nutrition, 92*(Supp. 2), 227-232.

Best, J. R. (2010). Effects of physical activity on children's executive function: Contributions of experimental research on aerobic exercise. *Developmental Review, 30*(4), 331-351. https://doi.org/10.1016/j.dr.2010.08.001

Biddle, S. J. H., Gorely, T., & Stensel, D. J. (2004). Health-enhancing physical activity and sedentary behaviour in children and adolescents. *Journal of Sports Sciences, 22*(8), 679-701. https://doi.org/10.1080/02640410410001712412

Biddulph, S. (1995). Foreword. In R. Browne & R. Fletcher (Eds.), *Boys in schools: addressing the real issues,* (pp.viii). Finch Publishing

Biddulph, S. (1998). *Raising boys.* Finch Publishing.

Biddulph, S. (2013). *The new manhood.* Simon & Schuster Australia.

Bilodeau, B. (2005). Beyond the gender binary: A case study of two transgender students at a mid-western research university. *Journal of Gay & Lesbian Issues in Education, 3*(1), 29-44. https://doi.org/10.1300/J367v03n01_05

Bjorklund, D. F., & Douglas Brown, R. (1998). Physical play and cognitive development: Integrating activity, cognition, and education. *Child Development, 69*(3), 604-606.

Blakemore, S. J. (2018). *Inventing ourselves: The secret life of the teenage brain.* PublicAffairs.

Blakemore, S. J., & Frith, U. (2005). *The learning brain: Lessons for education.* Blackwell Publishing.

Blakemore, S. J., & Choudhury, S. (2006). Development of the adolescent brain: Implications for executive function and social cognition. *Journal of Child Psychology and Psychiatry, 47*(3–4), 296–312. https://doi.org/10.1111/j.1469-7610.2006.01611.x

Blick-Hoyenga, K. & Hoyenga, K.T. (1993). *Gender related differences: Origins and outcomes.* Allyn & Bacon.

Blum, D. (1997). *Sex on the brain: The biological differences between men and women.* Penguin Books.

Bolton, R. (2019, December 3). Australian maths students fall years behind China. *Australian Financial Review.*

Borgonovi, F. (2016). Video gaming and gender differences in digital and printed reading performance among 15-year-olds students in 26 countries. *Journal of Adolescence, 48*, 45–61. https://doi.org/10.1016/j.adolescence.2016.01.004

Booker, C. L., Kelly, Y. J., & Sacker, A. (2018). Gender differences in the associations between age trends of social media interaction and well-being among 10-15-year-olds in the UK. *BMC Public Health, 18*, Article 321. https://doi.org/10.1186/s12889-018-5220-4

Bornstein, M. H., Hahn, C.-S., & Haynes, O. M. (2004). Specific and general language performance across early childhood: Stability and gender considerations. *First Language, 24*(3), 267–304. https://doi.org/10.1177/0142723704045681

Bornstein, M. H., Cote, L. R., Maital, S., Painter, K., Park, S.-Y., Pascual, L., Pêcheux, M.-G., Ruel, J., Venuti, P., & Vyt, A. (2004). Cross-linguistic analysis of vocabulary in young children: Spanish, Dutch, French, Hebrew, Italian, Korean, and American English. *Child Development, 75*(4), 1115–1139.

Bowlby, J. (1969). *Attachment and Loss, Volume 1: Attachment.* Basic Books.

Bransford, J. D., Brown, A. L., & Cocking, R. R. (2000). *How people learn: Brain, mind, experience and school.* National Academy Press.

Brizendine, L. (2006). *The female brain.* Morgan Road Books.

Brizendine, L. (2010). *The male brain: A breakthrough understanding of how men and boys think.* Broadway Books.

Brockmyer, J. F. (2015). Playing violent video games and desensitization to violence. *Child and Adolescent Psychiatric Clinics of North America, 24*(1), 65–77. https://doi.org/10.1016/j.chc.2014.08.001

Brooks, R. & Goldstein, S. (2001). *Raising resilient children.* Contemporary Books.

Brown, L. L. (2018). Intense romantic love uses subconscious survival circuits in the brain. In D. J. Linden (Ed.), *Think tank: Forty neuroscientists explore the roots of human experience* (pp. 208–214). Yale University Press.

Browne, R., & Fletcher, R. (1995). *Boys in schools: Addressing the real issues.* Finch Publishing.

Bruer, J. Y. (1999). Neural connections: Some you use, some you lose. *Phi Delta Kappan, 81*(4), 264–277.

Burdette, H. L., & Whitaker, R. C. (2005). Resurrecting free play in young children: Looking beyond fitness and fatness to attention, affiliation and affect. *Archives of Pediatric and Adolescent Medicine, 159*(1), 46–50. https://doi.org/10.1001/archpedi.159.1.46

Burman, D. D., Bitan, T., & Booth, J.R. (2008). Sex differences in neural processing of language among children. *Neuropsychologia, 46*(5), 1349–1362. https://doi.org/10.1016/j.neuropsychologia.2007.12.021

Cahill, L. (2005). His brain, her brain. *Scientific American, 292*(5), 40–47.

Caine, R.N. & Caine, G. (1994). *Making connections: Teaching and the Human Brain*. Addison Wesley Publishing Company.

Caine, G. & Caine, R.N. (2001). *The brain, education, and the competitive edge*. The Scarecrow Press Inc.

Canli, T., Desmond, J. E., Zhao, Z., & Gabrieli, J. D. E. (2002). Sex differences in the neural basis of emotional memories. *Proceedings of the National Academy of Sciences, 99*(16), 10789–10794. https://doi.org/10.1073/pnas.162356599

Carlson, N. R. (2000). *Physiology of behavior* (7th ed.). Allyn and Bacon.

Carnagey, N. L., Anderson, C. A., & Bushman, B. J. (2007). The effect of video game violence on physiological desensitization to real-life violence. *Journal of Experimental Social Psychology, 43*(3), 489–496. https://doi.org/10.1016/j.jesp.2006.05.003

Carson, V., Lee, E. Y., Hesketh, K. D., Hunter, S., Kuzik, N., Predy, M., Rhodes, R. E., Rinaldi, C. M., Spence, J. C., & Hinkley, T. (2019). Physical activity and sedentary behavior across three time-points and associations with social skills in early childhood. *BMC Public Health, 19*, Article 27. https://doi.org/10.1186/s12889-018-6381-x

Carter, R. (2000). *Mapping the mind*. Orion Books.

Casey, B. J., Jones, R. M., & Somerville, L. H. (2011). Braking and accelerating of the adolescent brain. *Journal of Research on Adolescence, 21*(1), 21–33. https://doi.org/10.1111/j.1532-7795.2010.00712.x

Ceci, S. J., Williams, W. M., & Barnett, S. M. (2009). Women's underrepresentation in science: Sociocultural and biological considerations. *Psychological Bulletin, 135*(2), 218–261. https://doi.org/10.1037/a0014412

Chaddock-Heyman, L., Hillman, C. H., Cohen, N. J., & Kramer, A. F. (2014). The importance of physical activity and aerobic fitness for cognitive control and memory in children. *Monographs of the Society for Research in Child Development, 79*(4), 25–50. https://doi.org/10.1111/mono.12129

Chapple, A. & Ziebland, S. (2004). The role of humour for men with testicular cancer. *Qualitative Health Research, 14*, 1123-1139.

Cheng, Y., Chou, K. H., Decety, J., Chen, I.-Y., Hung, D., Tzeng, O. J.-L., & Lin, C.-P. (2009). Sex differences in the neuroanatomy of human mirror-neuron system: A voxel-based morphometric investigation. *Neuroscience, 158*(2), 713–720. https://doi.org/10.1016/j.neuroscience.2008.10.026

Chipere, N. (2014). Sex differences in phonological awareness and reading ability. *Language Awareness, 23*(3), 275–289. https://doi.org/10.1080/09658416.2013.774007

Christodoulou, D. (2014). *Seven myths about education*. Routledge.

Chugani, H. T. (1994). Development of regional brain glucose metabolism in relation to behavior and plasticity. In G. Dawson & K. W. Fischer (Eds.), *Human behavior and the developing brain* (pp. 153–175). Guilford Publications.

Chugani, H. T. (1996). Neuroimaging of developmental non-linearity and developmental pathologies. In R. W. Thatcher, G. R. Lyon, J. Rumsey & N. Krasnegor (Eds). *Developmental neuroimaging: Mapping the development of brain and behavior* (pp. 187–195). Academic Press.

Chugani, H. T. (1998). Biological basis of emotions: Brain systems and brain development. *Pediatrics, 102*(5), 1225–1229.

Chugani, H. T., Phelps M. E., & Mazziotta J. C. (1987). Positron emission tomography study of human brain functional development. *Annals of Neurology, 22*(4), 487–497. https://doi.org/10.1002/ana.410220408

Chugani, H. T., Phelps M. E., & Mazziotta J. C. (1989). Metabolic assessment of functional maturation and neuronal plasticity in the human brain. In C. von Euler, C. Forssberg & H. Lagercrantz (Eds.), *Wenner-Gren international symposium series: Vol. 55. Neurobiology of early infant behaviour.* (pp. 323–330). Stockton Press.

Chugani, D. C., Muzik, O., Behen, M., Rothermel, R., Janisse, J. J., Lee, J., & Chugani, H. T. (1999). Developmental changes in brain serotonin synthesis capacity in autistic and nonautistic children. *Annals of Neurology, 45*(3), 287–295. https://doi.org/10.1002/1531-8249(199903)45:3<287::AID-ANA3>3.0.CO;2-9

Clements, A. M, Rimrodt, S. L., Abel, J. R., Blankner, J. G., Mostofsky, S. H., Pekar, J. J., Denckla, M. B., & Cutting, L.E. (2006). Sex differences in cerebral laterality of language and visuospatial processing. *Brain and Language, 98*(2), 150–158. https://doi.org/10.1016/j.bandl.2006.04.007

Coe, D. P., Pivarnik, J. M., Womack, C. J., Reeves, M. J., & Malina, R. M. (2006). Effect of physical education and activity levels on academic achievement in children. *Medicine & Science in Sports & Exercise, 38*(8), 1515–1519. https://doi.org/10.1249/01.mss.0000227537.13175.1b

Collaer, M. L., & Hines, M. (1995). Human behavioral sex differences: A role for gonadal hormones during early development? *Psychological Bulletin, 118*(1), 55–107. https://doi.org/10.1037/0033-2909.118.1.55

Collin, L., Reisner, S. L., Tangpricha, T., & Goodman, M. (2016). Prevalence of transgender depends on the "case" definition: A systematic review. *The Journal of Sexual Medicine, 13*(4), 613–626. https://doi.org/10.1016/j.jsxm.2016.02.001

Commission on Children at Risk. (2003). *Hardwired to connect: The new scientific case for authoritative communities. Institute for American Values.* http://americanvalues.org/catalog/pdfs/hwexsumm.pdf

Committee on Education and Training (2002). *Boys: Getting it right: Report on the inquiry into the education of boys.* Commonwealth of Australia. http://hdl.voced.edu.au/10707/112304.

Connell, R. W. (2000). *The men and the boys.* Allen & Unwin.

Connellan, J., Baron-Cohen, S., Wheelwright, S., Batki, A., & Ahluwalia, J. (2000). Sex differences in human neonatal social perception. *Infant Behavior & Development, 23*(1), 113–118. https://doi.org/10.1016/S0163-6383(00)00032-1

Costa, V. D., Lang, P. J., Sabatinelli, D., Versace, F., & Bradley, M. M. (2010). Emotional imagery: Assessing pleasure and arousal in the brain's reward circuitry. *Human Brain Mapping, 31*(9), 1446–1457. https://doi.org/10.1002/hbm.20948

Cooper, C. E., Osborne, C. A., Beck, A. N., & McLanahan, S. S. (2011). Partnership instability, school readiness and gender disparities. *Sociology of Education, 84*(3), 246–259. https://doi.org/10.1177/0038040711402361

Cozolino, L. (2013). *The social neuroscience of education: Optimizing attachment and learning in the classroom*. W. W. Norton & Company.

Cresswell, J., Rowe, K., & Withers, G. (2002). *Boys in school and society*. Australian Council for Educational Research.

Dahl, R. (2003). Beyond raging hormones: The tinderbox in the teenage brain. *Cerebrum, 5*(3), 7–22.

Dalley, J. W., & Roiser, J. P. (2012). Dopamine, serotonin and impulsivity. *Neuroscience, 215*(26), 42–58. https://doi.org/10.1016/j.neuroscience.2012.03.065

Damasio, A. R. (1994). *Descartes' error: Emotion, reason and the human brain*. Penguin.

Damasio, A. R. (2000). *The feeling of what happens: Body and emotion in the making of consciousness*. Harcourt.

Damasio, A. R. (2001). Emotion and the human brain. *Annals of the New York Academy of Sciences, 935*(1), 101–106.

Davis, C. L., Tomprowski, P. D., McDowell, J. E., Austin, B. P., Miller, P. H., Yanasak, N. E., Allison, J. D., & Naglieri, J. A. (2011). Exercise improves executive function and achievement and alters brain activation in overweight children: A randomized, controlled trial. *Health Psychology, 30*(1), 91–98. https://doi.org/10.1037/a0021766

De Bellis, M. D., Keshaven, M. S., Beers, S. R., Hall, J., Frustaci, K., Masalehdan, A., Noll, J., & Boring, A. M. (2001). Sex differences in brain maturation during childhood and adolescence. *Cerebral Cortex, 11*(6), 552–557. https://doi.org/10.1093/cercor/11.6.552

de Beauvoir, S. (2011). *The second sex* (C. Borde & S. Malovany-Chevallier, Trans.). Vintage Books. (Original work published 1949)

de Boise, S. (2019). Editorial: Is masculinity toxic? *NORMA: International Journal for Masculinity Studies, 14*(3), 147–151. https://doi.org/10.1080/18902138.2019.1654742

Del Giudice, M., Booth, T., & Irwing, P. (2012). The distance between Mars and Venus: Measuring global sex differences in personality. *PLOS One, 7*(1), Article e29265. https://doi.org/10.1371/journal.pone.0029265

Desai, R. A., Krishnan-Sarin, S., Cavallo, D., & Potenza, M. N. (2010). Video-gaming among high school students: Health correlates, gender differences, and problematic gaming. *Pediatrics, 126*(6), Article e1414-e1424. https://doi.org/10.1542/peds.2009-2706

Diamond, M., & Hopson, J. (1999). *Magic trees of the mind: How to nurture your child's intelligence, creativity, and healthy emotions from birth through adolescence*. Penguin Putnam.

Domes, G., Heinrichs, M., Glascher, J., Buchel, C., Braus, D. F., & Herpertz, S. (2007). Oxytocin attenuates amygdala responses to emotional faces regardless of valence. *Biological Psychiatry, 62*(10), 1187–1190. https://doi.org/10.1016/j.biopsych.2007.03.025

Dong, G., Wang, L., Du, X., & Potenza, M. N. (2018). Gender-related differences in neural processes to gaming cues before and after gaming: Implications for gender-specific vulnerabilities to internet gaming disorder. *Social Cognitive and Affective Neuroscience, 13*(11), 1203–1214. https://doi.org/10.1093/scan/nsy084

Dubb, A., Gur, R., Avants, B., & Gee, J. (2003). Characterization of sexual dimorphism in the human corpus callosum. *NeuroImage, 20*(1), 512–519. https://doi.org/10.1016/S1053-8119(03)00313-6

Eagleman, D. (2007, July 31). 10 unsolved mysteries of the brain: what we know – and don't know – about how we think. *Discover.* https://www.discovermagazine.com/mind/10-unsolved-mysteries-of-the-brain

Eliot, L. (2000). *What's going on in there? How the brain and mind develop in the first five years of life.* Bantam Books.

Eliot, L. (2012). *Pink brain, blue brain: How small differences grow into troublesome gaps and what we can do about it.* Oneworld Publications.

Eme, R. F. (2007). Sex differences in child-onset, life-course-persistent conduct disorder. A review of biological influences. *Clinical Psychology Review, 27*(5), 607–627. https://doi.org/10.1016/j.cpr.2007.02.001

Engelhardt, C. R., Bartholow, B. D., Kerr, G. T., & Bushman, B. J. (2011). This is your brain on violent video games: Neural desensitization to violence predicts increased aggression following violent video game exposure. *Journal of Experimental Social Psychology, 47*(5), 1033–1036. https://doi.org/10.1016/j.jesp.2011.03.027

Erickson, M., Marschik, P. B., Tulviste, T., Almgren, M. A., Pereira, M. G., Wehberg, S., Marjanovic-Umek, L., Gayraud, F., Kovacevic, M., & Gallego, C. (2012). Differences between girls and boys in emerging language skills: Evidence from 10 language communities. *British Journal of Developmental Psychology, 30*(2), 326–343. https://doi.org/10.1111/j.2044-835X.2011.02042.x

Fenson, L., Marchman, V. A., Thal, D. J., Dale, P., Reznick, S., & Bates, E. (2007). *Macarthur-Bates communicative development inventories* (2nd ed.). Brookes Publishing.

Finn, J. D., & Achilles, C. M. (1999). Tennessee's class size study: Findings, implications and misconceptions. *Educational Evaluation and Policy Analysis, 21*(2), 97–109. https://doi.org/10.3102/01623737021002097

Fischer, A. H., Kret, M. E., & Broekens, J. (2018). Gender differences in emotion perception and self-reported emotional intelligence: A test of the emotion sensitivity hypothesis. *PLOS One, 13*(1), Article e0190712. https://doi.org/10.1371/journal.pone.0190712

Ford, E. (1997). *Discipline for home and school: Book 1. Teaching children to respect the rights of others through responsible thinking based on perceptual control theory, revised and expanded edition.* Brandt Publishing.

Fox, S. E., Levitt, P., & Nelson, C. A. (2010). How the timing and quality of early experiences influence the development of brain architecture. *Child Development, 81*(1), 28–40. https://doi.org/10.1111/j.1467-8624.2009.01380.x

Galyan, D. (2001). Watching Star Trek with Dylan. In P. Stevens (Ed.), *Between mothers and sons: Women writers talk about having sons and raising men* (pp. 45–58). Scribner.

Garrett, B. (2009). *Brain and behavior: An introduction to biological psychology* (2nd ed.). Sage Publications.

Geake, J. G. (2009). *The brain at school: Educational neuroscience in the classroom.* Open University Press.

Geary, D. C. (2002). Sexual selection and sex differences in social cognition. In A. V. McGillicuddy-De Lisi & R. De Lisi (Eds.), *Biology, society and behavior: The development of sex differences in cognition* (pp. 23–53). Greenwood Publishing Group.

Geary, D. C. (2010). *Male, female: The evolution of human sex difference* (2nd ed.). American Psychological Association.

Gennetian, L. A. (2005). One or two parents? Half or step siblings? The effect of family structure on young children's achievement. *Journal of Population Economics, 18*(3), 415–436. https://doi.org/10.1007/s00148-004-0215-0

Giedd, J. N. (2004). Structural magnetic resonance imaging of the adolescent brain. *Annals of the New York Academy of Sciences, 1021*(1), 77–85. https://doi.org/10.1196/annals.1308.009

Giedd, J. N., Blumenthal, J., Jeffries, N. O., Castellanos, F. X., Liu, H., Zijdenbos, A., Paus, T., Evans, C., & Rapoport, J. L. (1999). Brain development during childhood and adolescence: A longitudinal MRI study. *Nature Neuroscience, 2*(10), 861–863. https://doi.org/10.1038/13158

Giedd, J. N, Clasen, L. S., Lenroot, R., Greenstein, D., Wallace, G. L., Ordaz, S., Molloy, E. A., Blumenthal, J. D., Tossell, J. W., Stayer, C., Samango-Sprouse, C. A., Shen, D., Davatzikos, C., Merke, D., & Chrousos, G. P. (2006). Puberty-related influences on brain development. *Molecular and Cellular Endocrinology, 254–255*, 154–162. https://doi.org/10.1016/j.mce.2006.04.016

Giedd, J. N., Vaituzis, C., Hamburger, S. D., Lange, N., Rajapakse, J. C., Kaysen, D., Vauss, Y. C., & Rapoport, J. L. (1996). Quantitative MRI of the temporal lobe, amygdala and hippocampus in normal human development: Ages 4–18 years. *Journal of Comparative Neurology, 366*(2), 223–230. https://doi.org/10.1002/(SICI)1096-9861(19960304)366:2<223::AID-CNE3>3.0.CO;2-7

Gilbert, R., & Gilbert, P. (1998). *Masculinity goes to school.* Allen and Unwin.

Ginsburg, H. P., & Opper, S. (1988). *Piaget's theory of intellectual development* (3rd ed.). Prentice-Hall.

Glasser, W. (1998). *Choice theory: A new psychology for personal freedom.* HarperCollins.

Gneezy, U., & Rustichini, A. (2004). Gender and competition at a younger age. *American Economic Review, 94*(2), 377–381. https://doi.org/10.1257/0002828041301821

Goldberg, E. (2001). *The executive brain: Frontal lobes and the civilized mind.* Oxford University Press.

Goldberg, E. (2009). *The new executive brain: Frontal lobes in a complex world.* Oxford University Press.

Goleman, D. (1995). *Emotional intelligence: Why it can matter more than IQ.* Bantam Books.

Goleman, D. (2006). *Social intelligence: Beyond IQ, beyond emotional intelligence.* Bantam Books.

Golinkoff, R. M., & Hirsch-Pasek, K. (2016). *Becoming brilliant: What science tells us about raising successful children.* American Psychological Association.

Gooren, L. (2006). The biology of human psychosexual differentiation. *Hormones and Behavior, 50*(4), 589–601. https://doi.org/10.1016/j.yhbeh.2006.06.011

Gopnik, A., Meltzoff, A. N., & Kuhl, P. K. (1999). *The scientist in the crib: What early learning tells us about the mind.* HarperCollins.

Goran, M. I., Nagy, T. T., Gower, B. A., Mazariegos, M., Solomons, N., Hood, V., & Johnson, R. (1998). Influence of sex, seasonality, ethnicity and geographic location on the components of total energy expenditure in young children: Implications for energy requirements. *The American Journal of Clinical Nutrition, 68*(3), 675–682. https://doi.org/10.1093/ajcn/68.3.675

Goyal, M. S., Blazey, T. M., Su, Y., Couture, L. E., Durbin, T. J., Bateman, R. J., Benzinger, T. L. S., Morris, J. C., Raichle, M. E., & Vlassenko, A. G. (2019). Persistent metabolic youth in the aging female brain. *Proceedings of the National Academy of Sciences, 116*(8), 3251–3255. https://doi.org/10.1073/pnas.1815917116

Graber, J. A., & Brooks-Gunn, J. (1998). Puberty. In E. A. Blechmnan & K. D Brownell (Eds.), *Behavioral medicine and women: A comprehensive handbook* (pp. 51–58). Guilford Press.

Gray, J. (1992). *Men are from Mars, women are from Venus.* HarperCollins.

Greitemeyer, T. (2014). Intense acts of violence during video game play make daily life aggression appear innocuous: A new mechanism why violent video games increase aggression. *Journal of Experimental Social Psychology, 50,* 52–56. https://doi.org/10.1016/j.jesp.2013.09.004

Greitemeyer, T., & Mügge, D. O. (2014). Video games do affect social outcomes: A meta-analytic review of the effects of violent and prosocial video game play. *Personality and Social Psychology Bulletin, 40*(5), 578–589. https://doi.org/10.1177/0146167213520459

Grimes, R. L. (2002). *Deeply into the bone: Re-inventing rites of passage.* University of California Press.

Grof, C. (1996). Rites of passage: A necessary step toward wholeness. In L. Carus-Mahdi, N. Geyer-Christopher & M. Meade (Eds.), *Crossroads: The quest for contemporary rites of passage* (pp. 3–16). Open Court Publishing Company.

Guiney, H., & Machado, L. (2013). Benefits of regular aerobic exercise for executive functioning in healthy populations. *Psychonomic Bulletin & Review, 20*(1), 73–86. https://doi.org/10.3758/s13423-012-0345-4

Gur, R. C., Gunning-Dixon, F., Bilker, W. B., & Gur, R. E. (2002). Sex differences in temporo-limbic and frontal brain volumes of healthy adults. *Cerebral Cortex, 12*(9), 998–1003. https://doi.org/10.1093/cercor/12.9.998

Gur, R. C., & Gur, R. E. (2017). Complementarity of sex difference in brain and behavior: From laterality to multi-modal neuroimaging. *Journal of Neuroscience Research, 95*(1–2), 189–199. https://doi.org/10.1002/jnr.23830

Gur, R. C., Mozley, L. H., Mozley, P. D., Resnick, S. M., Karp, J. S., Alavi, A., Arnold, S. E., & Gur, R. E. (1995). Sex differences in regional cerebral glucose metabolism during a resting state. *Science, 267*(5197), 528–531. https://doi.org/10.1126/science.7824953

Gur, R. C., Mozley, P. D., Resnick, S. M., Gottlieb, G. L., Kohn, M., Zimmerman, R., Herman, G., Atlas, S., Grossman, R., Berretta, D., Erwin, R., & Gur, R. E. (1991). Gender differences in age effect on brain atrophy measured by magnetic resonance imaging. *Proceedings of the National Academy of Sciences, 88*(7), 2845–2849.

Gur, R. C., Turetsky, B. I., Matsui, M., Yan, M., Bilker, W., Hughett, P., & Gur, R. E. (1999). Sex differences in brain gray matter and white matter in healthy young adults: Correlations with cognitive performance. *The Journal of Neuroscience, 19*(10), 4065–4072.

Gur, R. E., & Gur, R. C. (1990). Gender differences in cerebral blood flow. *Schizophrenia Bulletin, 16*(2), 247–254. https://doi.org/10.1093/schbul/16.2.247

Gurian, M. (*with Annis, B*). (2008). *Leadership and the sexes.* Jossey-Bass.

Gurian, M. & Ballew, A. C. (2003). *The boys and girls learn differently action guide for teachers.* Jossey-Bass.

Gurian, M. & Stevens, K. (2005). *The minds of boys: Saving our sons from falling behind in school and life.* Jossey-Bass.

Gurian, M. & Stevens, K. (2011). *Boys and girls learn differently! A guide for teachers and parents* (Revised 10th anniversary ed.). Jossey-Bass.

Gurian, M., Henley, P. & Trueman, T. (2001). *Boys and girls learn differently! A guide for teachers and parents.* Jossey-Bass.

Gurian, M., Stevens, K. & Daniels, P. (2009). *Successful single-sex classrooms: A practical guide to teaching boys and girls separately.* Jossey-Bass.

Haidt, J. (2012). *The righteous mind: Why good people are divided by politics and religion.* Vintage Books.

Haier, R. J., & Jung, R. E. (2008). Brain imaging studies of intelligence and creativity: What is the picture for education? *Roeper Review, 30*(3), 171–180. https://doi.org/10.1080/02783190802199347

Hall, G. S. (1904). *Adolescence: Its psychology and its relations to physiology, anthropology, sociology, sex, crime, religion, and education.* Appleton.

Hall, J.A., Carter, J.D. & Horgan, T.G. (2000). Gender differences in the nonverbal communication of emotion. In A.H. Fisher (Ed.), *Gender and Emotion: Social Psychological Perspectives*, (pp.97-117). Cambridge University Press.

Halpern, D. F. (2000). *Sex differences in cognitive abilities* (3rd ed.). Lawrence Erlbaum Associates.

Hanford-Morhard, R. (2013). *Wired to move: Facts and strategies for nurturing boys in an early childhood setting.* Gryphon House.

Hanlon, H. W. (1996). Topographically different regional networks impose structural limitations on both sexes. In K. H. Prilbram & J. King (Eds.), *Learning as self-organization* (pp. 311–378). Lawrence Erlbaum Associates.

Hannaford, C. (2005). *Smart moves: Why learning is not all in your head* (2nd ed.). Great River Books.

Harasty, J., Double, K. L., Halliday, G. M., Kril, J. J., & McRitchie, D. A. (1997). Language-associated cortical regions are proportionally larger in the female brain. *Archives of Neurology, 54*(2), 171–176. https://doi.org/10.1001/archneur.1997.00550140045011

Hardiman, M. M. (2003). *Connecting brain research with effective teaching: The brain-targeted teaching model.* Scarecrow Press.

Harper, C. C., & McLanahan, S. S. (2004). Father absence and youth incarceration. *Journal of Research on Adolescence, 14*(3), 369–397. https://doi.org/10.1111/j.1532-7795.2004.00079.x

Harris, J., Golinkoff, R. M., & Hirsh-Pasek, K. (2011). Lessons from the crib for the classroom: How children really learn vocabulary. In S. B. Neuman & D. K. Dickinson (Eds.), *Handbook of literacy research* (pp. 49-65). Guilford Press.

Hart, J. L., & Nagel, M. C. (2017). Including playful aggression in early childhood curriculum and pedagogy. *Australasian Journal of Early Childhood, 42*(1), 41-48. https://doi.org/10.23965/AJEC.42.1.05

Hart, J. L., & Tannock, M. T. (2013). Playful aggression in early childhood settings. *Children Australia, 38*(3), 106–114. https://doi.org/10.1017/cha.2013.14

Hawkes, T. (2001). *Boy oh boy: How to raise and educate boys.* Pearson Education.

Healy, J. M. (2004). *Your child's growing mind: Brain development and learning from birth to adolescence.* Broadway Books.

Hemovich, V., & Crano, W. D. (2009). Family structure and adolescent drug use: An exploration of single-parent families. *Substance Use & Misuse, 44*(14), 2099–2113. https://doi.org/10.3109/10826080902858375

Herdt, G. H. (1981). *Guardians of the flutes: Vol 1. Idioms of masculinity.* The University of Chicago Press.

Hermans, E. J., Ramsey, N. F., & van Honk, J. (2008). Exogenous testosterone enhances responsiveness to social threat in the neural circuitry of social aggression in humans. *Biological Psychiatry, 63*(3), 263–270. https://doi.org/10.1016/j.biopsych.2007.05.013

Herschkowitz, N., & Herschkowitz, E. C. (2004). *A good start to life: Understanding your child's brain and behavior from birth to age 6.* Dana Press.

Hewes, J., & McEwan, G. (2006). *Let the children play: Nature's answer to early learning.* Early Childhood Learning Knowledge Centre.

Hills, A. P., King, N. A., & Armstrong, T. P. (2007). The contribution of physical activity and sedentary behaviours to the growth and development of children and adolescents. *Sports Medicine, 37*(6), 533–545. https://doi.org/10.2165/00007256-200737060-00006

Hirsch, E,D. (2018). *Why knowledge matters: Rescuing our children from failed educational theories.* Harvard Education Press.

Hirsch-Pasek, K., Golinkoff, R. M., & Eyer, D. (2004). *Einstein never used flashcards: How our children really learn – and why they need to play more and memorize less.* Rodale.

Hirsch-Pasek, K., Golinkoff, R. M., Berk, L. E., & Singer, D. G. (2009). *A mandate for playful learning in preschool presenting the evidence.* Oxford University Press.

Hoff Sommers, C. (2013). *The war against boys: How misguided politics are harming our young men.* Simon & Schuster.

Howard, P. J. (2006). *The owner's manual for the brain: Everyday applications from mind-brain research* (3rd ed.). Bard Press.

Hoyenga, K. B., & Hoyenga, K. T. (1993). *Gender-related differences: Origins and outcomes.* Allyn and Bacon.

Huesmann, L. R. (2007). The impact of electronic media violence: Scientific theory and research. *Journal of Adolescent Health, 41*(6), S6–S13. https://doi.org/10.1016/j.jadohealth.2007.09.005

Huttenlocher, P. R. (1979). Synaptic density in human frontal cortex – developmental changes and effects of aging. *Brain Research, 163*(2), 195–205. https://doi.org/10.1016/0006-8993(79)90349-4

Huttenlocher, P. R., de Courten, C., Garey, L. J., & Van der Loos, H. (1982). Synaptogenesis in human visual cortex--evidence for synapse elimination during normal development. *Neuroscience Letters, 33*(3), 247–52. https://doi.org/10.1016/0304-3940(82)90379-2

Hutton, J. S., Dudley, J., Horowitz-Kraus, T., DeWitt, T., & Holland, S. (2020). Associations between screen-based media use and brain white matter integrity in preschool-aged children. *Jama Pediatrics, 174*(1), Article e193869. https://doi.org/10.1001/jamapediatrics.2019.3869

Hyde, J. S., & Linn, M. C. (2006). Gender similarities in mathematics and science. *Science, 314*(5799), 599–600. https://doi.org/10.1126/science.1132154

Ingalhalikar, M., Smith, A., Parker, D., Satterthwaite, T. D., Elliott, M. A., Ruparel, K., Hakonarson, H., Gur, R. E., Gur, R. C., & Verma, R. (2014). Sex differences in the structural connectome of the human brain. *Proceedings of the National Academy of Sciences, 111*(2), 823–828. https://doi.org/10.1073/pnas.1316909110

Ives-Deliperi, V. L., Solms, M., & Meintjes, E. M. (2011). The neural substrates of mindfulness: An fMRI investigation. *Social Neuroscience, 6*(3), 231–242. https://doi.org/10.1080/17470919.2010.513495

James, A. N. (2007). *Teaching the male brain: How boys think, feel and learn in school.* Corwin Press.

Jarvis, P. (2006). "Rough and tumble" play: Lessons in life. *Evolutionary Psychology, 4*(1), 330–346. https://doi.org/10.1177/147470490600400128

Jensen, E. (2003). *Environments for learning.* Corwin.

Jha, A. P., Krompinger, J., & Baime, M. J. (2007). Mindfulness training modifies subsystems of attention. *Cognitive, Affective & Behavioral Neuroscience, 7*(2), 109–119. https://doi.org/10.3758/CABN.7.2.109

Johnston, T. (2008, February 8). An out-of-control party brings an Australian teenager to international fame. *The New York Times.* https://www.nytimes.com/2008/01/28/world/asia/28iht-party.1.9543375.html

Kalnin, A. J., Edwards, C. R., Wang, Y., Kronenberger, W. G., Hummer, T. A., Mosier, K. M., Dunn, D. W., & Matthews, V. P. (2011). The interacting role of media violence exposure and aggressive–disruptive behavior in adolescent brain activation during an emotional Stroop task. *Psychiatry Research: Neuroimaging, 192*(1), 12–19. https://doi.org/10.1016/j.pscychresns.2010.11.005

Kansaku, K., & Kitazawa, S. (2001). Imaging studies on sex differences in lateralization of language. *Neuroscience Research, 41*(4), 333–337. https://doi.org/10.1016/S0168-0102(01)00292-9

Kanasaku, K., Yamamura, A., & Kitazawa, S. (2000). Sex differences in lateralization revealed in the posterior language areas. *Cerebral Cortex, 10*(9), 866–872. https://doi.org/10.1093/cercor/10.9.866

Kardaras, N. (2016). *Glow kids: How screen addiction is hijacking our kids and how to break the trance.* St. Martin's Griffin.

Kearney, P. (2007). Cognitive assessment of game-based learning. *British Journal of Educational Technology, 38*(3), 529–531. https://doi.org/10.1111/j.1467-8535.2007.00718.x

Kimbrough, A. M., Guadango, R. E., Muscanell, N. L., & Dill, J. (2013). Gender differences in mediated communication: Women connect more than men do. *Computers in Human Behavior, 29*(3), 896–900. https://doi.org/10.1016/j.chb.2012.12.005

Kimura, D. (1999). *Sex and cognition.* MIT Press.

Kimura, D. (2004). Human sex differences in cognition: Fact, not predicament. *Sexualities, Evolution & Gender, 6*(1), 45–53. https://doi.org/10.1080/14616660410001733597

Kindlon, D. & Thompson, M. (1999). *Raising Cain: Protecting the emotional life of boys.* Ballantine Books

Király, A., Szabó, N., Tóth, E., Csete, G., Faragó, P., Kocsis, K., Must, A., Vécsei, L., & Kincses, Z. T. (2016). Male brains age faster: The age and gender dependence of subcortical volumes. *Brain Imaging and Behavior, 10*(3), 901–910. https://doi.org/10.1007/s11682-015-9468-3

Kirillova, G.P. (2003). Salivary cortisol, personality, and aggressive behavior in adolescent boys: a 5-year longitudinal study. *Journal of the American Academy of Child and Adloscent Psychiatry, 42(9), 1101-1108.*

Kiselica, M.S. (2003). Transforming psychotherapy in order to succeed with adolescent boys: Male-friendly practices. *Journal of Clinical Psychology, 59*(11), 1225–1236. https://doi.org/10.1002/jclp.10213

Kiselica, M. S., & Englar-Carlson, M. (2010). Identifying, affirming, and building upon male strengths: The positive psychology/positive masculinity model of psychotherapy with boys and men. *Psychotherapy: Theory, Research, Practice, Training, 47*(3), 276–287. https://doi.org/10.1037/a0021159

Kiselica, M. S., Englar-Carlson, M., Horne, A. M., & Fisher, M. (2008). A positive psychology perspective on helping boys. In M. S. Kiselica, M. Englar-Carlson & A. M. Horne (Eds.), *Counseling troubled boys: A guidebook for professionals* (pp. 31–48). Routledge.

Kong, X. Z., Mathias, S. R., Guadalupe, T., ENIGMA Laterality Working Group, Glahn, D. C., Franke, B., Crivello, F., Tzourio-Mazoyer, N., Fisher, S. E., Thompson, P. M., & Francks, C. (2018). Mapping cortical brain asymmetry in 17,141 healthy individuals worldwide via the ENIGMA Consortium. *Proceedings of the National Academy of Sciences, 22*, E5154–E5163. https://doi.org/10.1073/pnas.1718418115

Koolshijn, P. C. M. P., & Crone, E. A. (2013). Sex differences and structural brain maturation from childhood to early adulthood. *Developmental Cognitive Neuroscience, 5*, 106–118. https://doi.org/10.1016/j.dcn.2013.02.003

Kret, M. E., & De Gelder, B. (2012). A review on sex differences in processing emotional signals. *Neuropsychologia, 50*(7), 1211–1121. https://doi.org/10.1016/j.neuropsychologia.2011.12.022

Kuhl, P. K. (2010). Brain mechanisms in early language acquisition. *Neuron, 67*(5), 713–727. https://doi.org/10.1016/j.neuron.2010.08.038

Lai, C., Pellicano, G. R., Altavilla, D., Proietti, A., Lucarelli, G., Massaro, G., Luciani, M., & Aceto, P. (2019). Violence in video game produces a lower activation of limbic and temporal areas in response to social inclusion images. *Cognitive Affective & Behavioral Neuroscience, 19*(4), 898–909. https://doi.org/10.3758/s13415-018-00683-y

Lamb, M. E. (Ed.). (2010). *The role of the father in child development.* John Wiley & Sons.

Lane, R. D., & Nadel, L. (Eds). (2002). *Cognitive neuroscience of emotion.* Oxford University Press.

Lau, M., & Cline, H. (2018). How you use your brain can change its basic structural organization. In D. J. Linden (Ed.), *Think tank: Forty neuroscientists explore the roots of human experience* (pp. 52–59). Yale University Press.

LeDoux, J. (1998). *The emotional brain: The mysterious underpinnings of emotional life.* Simon & Schuster.

LeDoux, J. (2002). *The synaptic self: How our brains become who we are.* Penguin Books.

Lee, P. J. (2004). *Re-visioning adolescence and the rite of passage.* BookSurge.

Legato, M. J. (2002). *Eve's rib: The groundbreaking guide to women's health.* Three Rivers Press.

Legato, M. J. (2005). *Why men never remember and women never forget.* Rodale Books.

Lever, J. (1976). Sex differences in the games children play. *Social Problems, 23*(4), 478–487. https://doi.org/10.1525/sp.1976.23.4.03a00100

Lewis, R. (1997). *Raising a modern day knight: A father's role in guiding his son to authentic manhood.* Tyndale House Publishers.

Lidow, M. S., Goldman-Rakic, P. S., & Rakic, P. (1991). Synchronized overproduction of neurotransmitter receptors in diverse regions of the primate cerebral cortex. *Proceedings of the National Academy of Sciences, 88*(22), 10218–10221. https://doi.org/10.1073/pnas.88.22.10218

Lim, S., Han, C. E., Uhlhaas, P. J., & Kaiser, M. (2015). Preferential detachment during human brain development: Age and sex specific structural connectivity in diffusion tensor imaging (DTI) data. *Cerebral Cortex, 25*(6), 1477–1489. https://doi.org/10.1093/cercor/bht333

Linden, D. J. (2018a). Human sexual orientation is strongly influenced by biological factors. In D. J. Linden (Ed.), *Think tank: Forty neuroscientists explore the roots of human experience* (pp. 215–224). Yale University Press.

Linden, D. J. (2018b). Our human brain was not designed all at once by a genius inventor on a blank sheet of paper. In D. J. Linden (Ed.), *Think tank: Forty neuroscientists explore the roots of human experience* (pp. 1–8). Yale University Press.

Lindenfors, P., Nunn, C. L., & Barton, R. A. (2007). Primate brain architecture and selection in relation to sex. *BMC Biology, 5*, Article 20. https://doi.org/10.1186/1741-7007-5-20

Lissak, G. (2018) Adverse physiological and psychological effects of screen time on children and adolescents: Literature review and case study. *Environmental Research, 164*, 149–157. https://doi.org/10.1016/j.envres.2018.01.015

Loane, S. (1995, August 19). The trouble with boys. *Sydney Morning Herald.*

Lungu, O., Potvin, S., Tikàsz, A., & Mendrek, A. (2015). Sex differences in effective fronto-limbic connectivity during negative emotion processing. *Psychoneuroendocrinology, 62,* 180–188. https://doi.org/10.1016/j.psyneuen.2015.08.012

Lutchmaya, S., & Baron-Cohen, S. (2002). Human sex differences in social and non-social looking preferences, at 12 months of age. *Infant Behavior & Development, 25*(3), 319–325. https://doi.org/10.1016/S0163-6383(02)00095-4

Maccoby, E. E. (1998). *The two sexes: Growing up apart, coming together.* Harvard University Press.

Mann, J. J. (2013). The serotonergic system in mood disorders and suicidal behaviour. *Philosophical Transactions of the Royal Society B, 368*(1615), Article 20120537. https://doi.org/10.1098/rstb.2012.0537

Manocha, R. (2013). *Silence your mind: The new scientifically proven approach to meditation that will enhance your well-being & performance in just 10 minutes a day.* Hachette Australia.

Marcus, G. (2004). *The birth of a mind: How a tiny number of genes creates the complexities of human thought.* Basic Books.

Martin, C. L., & Fabes, R. A. (2001). The stability and consequences of young children's same-sex peer interactions. *Developmental Psychology, 37*(3), 431–446. https://doi.org/10.1037/0012-1649.37.3.431

Matsuda, G., & Hiraki, K. (2006). Sustained decreases in oxygenated hemoglobin during video games in the dorsal prefrontal cortex: A NIRS study of children. *NeuroImage, 29*(3), 706–711. https://doi.org/10.1016/j.NeuroImage.2005.08.019

Mason, P. (2018). We are born to help others. In D. J. Linden (Ed.), *Think tank: Forty neuroscientists explore the roots of human experience* (pp. 201–207). Yale University Press.

McCann, R. (2000). *On their own: Boys growing up under-fathered.* Finch Publishing.

McClure, E. B. (2000). A meta-analytic review of sex differences in facial expression processing and their development in infants, children and adolescents. *Psychological Bulletin, 126*(3), 424–453. https://doi.org/10.1037/0033-2909.126.3.424

McClure, E. B., Monk, C. S., Nelson, E. E., Zarahn, E., Leibenluft, E., Bilder, R. M., Charney, D. S., Ernst, M., & Pine, D. S. (2004). A developmental examination of gender differences in brain engagement during evaluation of threat. *Biological Psychiatry, 55*(11), 1047–1055. https://doi.org/10.1016/j.biopsych.2004.02.013

McEwen, B. S., & Seeman, T. (2003). Stress and affect: Applicability of the concepts of allostasis and allostatic load. In R. J. Davidson, K. R. Scherer & H. H. Goldsmith (Eds.), *Series in affective science. Handbook of affective sciences* (pp. 1117–1137). Oxford University Press.

McFadden, D. (1998). Sex differences in the auditory system. *Developmental Neuropsychology, 14*(2–3), 261–298. https://doi.org/10.1080/87565649809540712

McFarland, L., Murray, E., & Phillipson, S. (2016). Student–teacher relationships and student self-concept: Relations with teacher and student gender. *Australian Journal of Education, 60*(1), 5–25. https://doi.org/10.1177/0004944115626426

McGuire, A. (2017). *Sex scandal: The drive to abolish male and female.* Regnery Publishing.

McLanahan, S., Tach, L., & Schneider, D. (2013). The causal effects of father absence. *Annual Review of Sociology, 39*, 399–427. https://doi.org/10.1146/annurev-soc-071312-145704

Medina, J. (2010). *Brain rules for baby: How to raise a smart and happy child from zero to five.* Pear Press.

Meneses, A., & Liy-Salmeron, G. (2012). Serotonin and emotion, learning and memory. *Reviews in the Neurosciences, 23*(5–6), 543–553. https://doi.org/10.1515/revneuro-2012-0060

Miller, L., Balodis, I. M., McClintock, C. H., Xu, J., Lacadie, C. M., Sinha, R., & Potenza, M. N. (2019). Neural correlates of personalized spiritual experiences. *Cerebral Cortex, 29*(6), 2331–2338. https://doi.org/10.1093/cercor/bhy102

Minton, H. L. (1997). Queer theory: Historical roots and implications for psychology. *Theory & Psychology, 7*(3), 337–353. https://doi.org/10.1177/0959354397073003

Mitchell, K. J. (2018). *Innate: How the wiring of our brains shapes who we are.* Princeton University Press.

Mohandas, E. (2008). Neurobiology of spirituality. *Mens Sana Monographs, 6*(1), 63–80. https://doi.org/10.4103/0973-1229.33001

Moir, A., & Jessel, D. (1998). *Brain sex: The real difference between men and women.* Arrow Books.

Moir, A., & Moir, B. (1999). *Why men don't iron: The fascinating and unalterable differences between men and women.* Citadel Press.

Mol, S. E., & Bus, A. G. (2011). To read or not to read: A meta-analysis of print exposure from infancy to early adulthood. *Psychological Bulletin, 137*(2), 267–296. https://doi.org/10.1037/a0021890

Moloney, J. (2000). *Boys and books: Building a culture of reading around our boys.* ABC Books.

Mosteller, F. (1995). The Tennessee study of class size in the early school grades. *The Future of Children, 5*(2), 113–126.

Muller, C. P., & Jacobs, B. L. (Eds). (2010). *Handbook of behavioral neuroscience: Vol. 21. Handbook of the behavioral neurobiology of serotonin.* Elsevier.

Nadeau, R. L. (1996). *S/he brain: Science, sexual politics, and the myths of feminism.* Praeger Publishers.

Nagel, M. C. (2001). Quality time: Filling a student void. *Practising Administrator, 23*(4), 42–44.

Nagel, M. C. (2003). A quality approach to quality time. *Practising Administrator, 25*(3), 30–32.

Nagel, M. C. (2006). *Boys-stir-us: Working with the hidden nature of boys.* Hawker Brownlow Education.

Nagel, M. C. (2012). *In the beginning: The brain, early development and learning.* Australian Council for Educational Research (ACER).

Nagel, M. C. (2014). *In the middle: The adolescent brain, behaviour and learning.* Australian Council for Educational Research (ACER).

Nagel, M. C. (2019). Understanding learning and learners. In R. Churchill, S. Godinho, N. F. Johnson, A. Keddie, W. Letts, K. Lowe, J. McKay, M. McGill, J. Moss, M. C. Nagel, K. Shaw & J. Rogers (Eds). *Teaching: Making a difference* (4th ed., pp. 80–117). John Wiley & Sons.

Nagel, M. C. (2021). *It's a girl thing: Understanding the neuroscience behind educating and raising girls.* Melbourne: Amba Press.

Nagel, M. C., & Scholes, L. (2016). *Understanding development and learning: Implications for teaching.* Oxford University Press.

Nagy, E., Loveland, K. A., Orvos, H., & Molnár, P. (2001). Gender-related physiological differences in human neonates and the greater vulnerability of males to developmental brain disorders. *Journal of Gender-Specific Medicine, 4*(1), 41–49.

Neall, L. (2002). *Bringing out the best in boys: Communication strategies for teachers.* Hawthorn Press.

Nota, N. M., Kreukels, B. P. C., den Heijer, M., Veltman, D. J., Cohen-Kettenis, P. T., Burke, S. M., & Bakker, J. (2017). Brain functional connectivity patterns in children and adolescents with gender dysphoria: Sex-atypical or not? *Psychoneuroendocrinology, 86*, 187–195.

Organisation for Economic Co-operation and Development. (2010). *PISA 2009 results: Learning trends* (Changes in Student Performance Since 2000, Vol. 5). OECD Publishing. https://doi.org/10.1787/9789264091580-en

Organisation for Economic Co-operation and Development. (2014). *PISA 2012 results: What students know and can do* (Student Performance in Mathematics, Reading and Science, Vol. 1, Revised ed.). OECD Publishing. https://doi.org/10.1787/9789264208780-en

Organisation for Economic and Co-operation and Development. (2015a). *The ABC of gender equality in education: Aptitude, behaviour, confidence.* OECD Publishing.

Organisation for Economic and Co-operation and Development. (2015b). *Education at a glance 2015: OECD indicators.* OECD Publishing.

Organisation For Economic Co-operation and Development (2015c). *Students, computers and learning: Making the connection*. OECD Publishing.

Organisation For Economic Co-operation and Development (2019). *PISA 2018 assessment and analytical framework*. OECD Publishing.

Owen, A. M., Hampshire, A., Grahn, J. A., Stenton, R., Dajani, S., Burns, A. S., Howard, R. J., & Ballard, C. G. (2010). Putting brain training to the test. *Nature, 465*(7299) 775–778. https://doi.org/10.1038/nature09042

Panksepp, J. (2005). *Affective neuroscience: The foundations of human and animal emotions*. Oxford University Press.

Panksepp, J., & Biven, L. (2012). *The archeology of the mind: Neuroevolutionary origins of human emotions*. W. W. Norton & Company.

Pascual-Leone, A., Amedi, A., Fregni, F., & Merabet, L. B. (2005). The plastic human cortex. *Annual Review of Neuroscience, 28*, 377–401. https://doi.org/10.1146/annurev.neuro.27.070203.144216

Pashler, H., McDaniel, M., Rohrer, D., & Bjork, R. (2008). Learning styles: Concepts and evidence. *Psychological Science in the Public Interest, 9*(3), 105–119. https://doi.org/10.1111/j.1539-6053.2009.01038.x

Peiper, A. (1925). Sinnesempfindungen des Kindes vor seiner Geburt. *Monatsschrift fur Kinderheilkunde, 29*, 236–241.

Pellegrini, A. D., & Smith, P. K. (1998). Physical activity play: The nature and function of a neglected aspect of play. *Child Development, 69*(3), 577–598.

Pellegrini, A. D., Long, J. D., Roseth, C. J., Bohn, C. M., & Van Ryzin, M. (2007). A short-term longitudinal study of preschoolers' (Homo sapiens) sex segregation: The role of physical activity, sex, and time. *Journal of Comparative Psychology, 121*(3), 282–289. https://doi.org/10.1037/0735-7036.121.3.282

Peterson, J. B. (2018). *12 rules for life: An antidote to chaos*. Random House Canada.

Phillips, M. D., Lowe, M. J., Lurito, J. T., Dzemidzic, M., & Mathews, V. P. (2001). Temporal lobe activation demonstrates sex-based differences during passive listening. *Radiology, 220*(1), 202–207. https://doi.org/10.1148/radiology.220.1.r01jl34202

Piaget, J. (1928). *Judgment and reasoning in the child*. Routledge & Kegan Paul.

Piaget, J. (1953). *Origins of intelligence in the child*. Routledge & Kegan Paul.

Piaget, J. (1954). *Construction of reality in the child*. Routledge & Kegan Paul.

Piaget, J. (1971). *Science of education and the psychology of the child*. Longman Books.

Pinker, S. (2002). *The blank slate: The modern denial of human nature*. Penguin Books.

Pinker, S. (2007). *The language instinct: How the mind creates language*. Harper Perennial Modern Classics.

Pinker, S. (2009). *How the mind works*. W. W. Norton & Company.

Plato (2016). *The complete works of Plato (unabridged): From the greatest Greek philosopher, known for The Republic, Symposium, Apology, Phaedrus, Laws, Crito, Phaedo, Timaeus, Meno, Euthyphro, Gorgias, Parmenides, Protagoras, Statesman and Critias* (B. Jowlett, Trans.). e-artnow.

Pollack, W. (1998). *Real boys: Rescuing our sons from the myths of boyhood*. Scribe Publications.

Pomerantz, E. M., Altermatt, E. R., & Saxon, J. L. (2002). Making the grade but feeling distressed: Gender differences in academic performance and internal distress. *Journal of Educational Psychology, 94*(2), 396–404. https://doi.org/10.1037/0022-0663.94.2.396

Popenoe, D. (2017). *War over the family*. Routledge.

Pougnet, E., Serbin, L. A., Stack, D. M., & Schwartzman, A. E. (2011). Fathers' influence on children's cognitive and behavioural functioning: A longitudinal study of Canadian Families. *Canadian Journal of Behavioural Science, 43*(3), 173–82. https://doi.org/0.1037/a0023948

Price-Mohr, R., & Price, C. (2017). Gender differences in early reading strategies: A comparison of synthetic phonics only with a mixed approach to teaching reading to 4–5-year-old children. *Early Childhood Education Journal, 45*(5), 613–620. https://doi.org/10.1007/s10643-016-0813-y

Purves, D., Augustine, G. J., Fitzpatrick, D., Hall, W. C., LaMantia, A. S., McNamara, J. O., & White, L. E. (Eds.). (2008). *Neuroscience* (4th ed.). Sinauer Associates.

Raichle, M. E., & Gusnard, D. A. (2002). Appraising the brain's energy budget. *Proceedings of the National Academy of Sciences of the USA, 99*(16), 10237–10239. https://doi.org/10.1073/pnas.172399499

Rajan, V., Konishi, H., Ridge, K., Houston, D. M., Golinkoff, R. M., Hirsch-Pasek, K., Eastman, N., & Schwartz, R. G. (2019). Novel word learning at 21 months predicts receptive vocabulary outcomes in later childhood. *Journal of Child Language, 46*(4), 617–631. https://doi.org/10.1017/S0305000918000600

Raman, I. A. (2018). Like it or not, the brain grades on a curve. In D. J. Linden (Ed.), *Think tank: Forty neuroscientists explore the roots of human experience* (pp. 75–81). Yale University Press.

Ratey, J. J. (2001). *A user's guide to the brain: Perception, attention and the four theatres of the brain*. Vintage Books.

Ratey, J. J. (2008). *Spark: The revolutionary new science of exercise and the brain*. Little, Brown and Company.

Richardson, J. T. E. (1997). Conclusions from the study of gender differences in cognition. In J. Caplan, M. Crawford, J. Shibley-Hyde & J. T. E. Richardson (Eds.), *Gender differences in human cognition* (pp. 131–169). Oxford University Press.

Riener, C., & Willingham, D. (2010). The myth of learning styles. *Change: The Magazine of Higher Learning, 42*(5), 32–35. https://doi.org/10.1080/00091383.2010.503139

Ritchie, S. J., Cox, S. R., Shen, X., Lombardo, M. V., Reus, L. M., Alloza, C., Harris, M. A., Alderson, H. L., Hunter, S., Neilson, E., Liewald, D. C. M., Auyeung, B., Whalley, H. C., Lawrie, S. M., Gale, C. R., Bastin, M. E., McIntosh, A. M., & Deary, I. J. (2018). Sex differences in the adult human brain: Evidence from 5216 UK Biobank participants. *Cerebral Cortex, 28*(8), 2959–2975. https://doi.org/10.1093/cercor/bhy109

Rodriguez, E. T., Tamis-LeMonda, C. S., Spellman, M. E., Pan, B. A., Raikes, H., Lugo-Gil, J., & Luze, G. (2009). The formative role of home literacy experiences across the first three years of life in children from low-income families. *Journal of Applied Developmental Psychology, 30*(6), 677–694. https://doi.org/10.1016/j.appdev.2009.01.003

Rosales, F. J., Reznick, J. S., & Zeisel, S. H. (2009). Understanding the role of nutrition in the brain and behavioral development of toddlers and preschool children: Identifying and addressing methodological barriers. *Nutritional Neuroscience: An International Journal of Nutrition, Diet and the Nervous System, 12*(5), 190–202. https://doi.org/10.1179/147683009X423454

Rosso, I. M., Young, A. D., Femia, L. A., & Yurgelun-Todd, D. A. (2004). Cognitive and emotional components of frontal lobe functioning in childhood and adolescence. *Annals of the New York Academy of Sciences, 1021*(1), 355–362. https://doi.org/10.1196/annals.1308.045

Rubinstein, A. (2013). *The making of men: Raising boys to be happy, healthy and successful.* Brio Books.

Ruigrok, A. N. V., Salimi-Khorshidi, G., Lai, M. C., Baron-Cohen, S., Lombardo, M. V., Tait, R. J., & Suckling, J. (2014). A meta-analysis of sex differences in human brain structure. *Neuroscience and Biobehavioral Reviews, 39*, 34–50. https://doi.org/10.1016/j.neubiorev.2013.12.004

Sabatinelli, D., Lang, P. J., Bradley, M. M., Costa, V. D., & Versace, F. (2007). Pleasure rather than salience activates human nucleus accumbens and medial prefrontal cortex. *Journal of Neurophysiology, 98*(9), 1374–1379. https://doi.org/10.1152/jn.00230.2007

Sahlberg, P. (2010). *Finnish lessons: What can the world learn from educational change in Finland?* Teachers College Press.

Sapolsky, R. M. (1997). *The trouble with testosterone and other essays on the biology of the human predicament.* Scribner.

Sapolsky, R. M. (2017). *Behave: The biology of humans at our best and worst.* Penguin Books.

Saraswat, A., Weinand, J., & Safer, J. (2015) Evidence supporting the biologic nature of gender identity. *Endocrine Practice, 21*(2), 199–204. https://doi.org/10.4158/EP14351.RA

Savage, B.M., Lujan, H.L., Thipparthi, R.R. & DiCarlo, S.E. (2017). Humor, laughter, learning and health! A brief review. *Advances in Physiology Education, 41*(3), 341–347.

Savic, I., Garcia-Falgueras, A., & Swaab, D. F. (2010). Sexual differentiation of the human brain in relation to gender identity and sexual orientation. *Progress in Brain Research, 186*(4), 41–62. https://doi.org/10.1016/B978-0-444-53630-3.00004-X

Sax, L. (2002). How common is intersex? A response to Anne Fausto-Sterling. *The Journal of Sex Research, 39*(3), 174–178. https://doi.org/10.1080/00224490209552139

Sax, L. (2005). *Why gender matters: What parents and teachers need to know about the emerging science of sex differences.* Doubleday.

Sax, L. (2007). *Boys adrift: The five factors driving the growing epidemic of unmotivated boys and underachieving young men.* Basic Books.

Sax, L. (2017). *Why gender matters: What parents and teachers need to know about the emerging science of sex differences* (2nd ed.). Harmony Books.

Saylik, R., Raman, E., & Szameitat, A. J. (2018). Sex differences in emotion recognition and working memory tasks. *Frontiers in Psychology, 9*, 1072. https://doi.org/10.3389/fpsyg.2018.01072

Schanzenbach, D. W. (2006). What have researchers learned from Project STAR? *Brookings Papers on Education Policy, 9*, 205–228.

Schenck, J. (2011). *Teaching and the adolescent brain: An educator's guide.* W. W. Norton & Company.

Schneider, F., Habel, U., Kessler, C., Salloum, J. B., & Posse, S. (2000). Gender differences in regional cerebral activity during sadness. *Human Brain Mapping, 9*(4), 226–238. https://doi.org/10.1002/(SICI)1097-0193(200004)9:4<226::AID-HBM4>3.0.CO;2-K

Scholes, L. (2017). Books are boring! Books are fun! Boys' polarized perspectives on reading. *Boyhood Studies: An Interdisciplinary Journal, 11*(2), 77–98

Scholes, L. (2018). Working-class boys' relationships with reading: Contextual systems that support working-class boys' engagement with, and enjoyment of, reading. *Gender and Education, 31*(3), 344–361. https://doi.org/10.1080/09540 253.2018.1533921

Schulte-Rüther, M., Markowitsch, H. J., Jon Shah, N., Fink, G. R., & Piefke, M. (2008). Gender differences in brain networks supporting empathy. *NeuroImage, 42*(1), 393–403. https://doi.org/10.1016/j.NeuroImage.2008.04.180

Scott, E., & Panksepp, J. (2003). Rough-and-tumble play in human children. *Aggressive Behavior, 29*(6), 539–551. https://doi.org/10.1002/ab.10062

Seeman, P. (1999). Images in neuroscience: Brain development, X: Pruning during development. *American Journal of Psychiatry, 156*(2), 168.

Shamay-Tsoory, S. G., Aharon-Peretz, J., & Perry, D. (2009). Two systems for empathy: A double disassociation between emotional and cognitive empathy in inferior frontal gyrus versus ventromedial prefrontal lesions. *Brain, 132*(3), 617–627. https://doi.org/10.1093/brain/awn279

Shaywitz, B. A., Shaywitz, S. E., Pugh, K. R., Constable, R. T., Skudlarski, P., Fulbright, R. K., Bronen, R. A., Fletcher, J. M., Shankweiler, D. P., Katz, L., & Gore, J. C. (1995). Sex differences in the functional organization of the brain for language. *Nature, 373*(6515), 607–609. https://doi.org/10.1038/373607a0

Shin, Y. W., Kim, D. J., Hyon, T., Park, H. J., Moon, W. J., Chung, E. C., Lee, J. M., Kim, I. Y., Kim, S. I., & Kwon, J. S. (2005). Sex differences in the human corpus callosum: Diffusion tensor imaging study. *NeuroReport, 16*(8), 795–798. https://doi.org/10.1097/00001756-200505310-00003

Shonkoff, J. P., & Phillips, D. A. (Eds.). (2000). *From neurons to neighborhoods: The science of early childhood development.* National Academy Press.

Sigmundsson, H., Eriksen, A. D., Ofteland, G. S., & Haga, M. (2017). Letter-sound knowledge: Exploring gender differences in children when they start school regarding knowledge of large letters, small letters, sound large letters and sound small letters. *Frontiers in Psychology, 8,* 1539. https://doi.org/10.3389/fpsyg.2017.01539

Singer, G., & Revensen, T. A. (1996). *A Piaget primer: How a child thinks, revised edition.* Penguin Books.

Sisk, C. L., & Foster, D. L. (2004). The neural basis of puberty and adolescence. *Nature Neuroscience, 7*(10), 1040–1047. https://doi.org/10.1038/nn1326

Sowell, E. R., Thompson, P. M., Holmes, C. J., Jernigan, T. I., & Toga, A. W. (1999). In vivo evidence for post-adolescent brain maturation in frontal and striatal regions. *Nature Neuroscience, 2*(10), 859–861. https://doi.org/10.1038/13154

Spalek, K., Fastenrath, M., Ackermann, S., Auschra, B., Coynel, D., Frey, J., Gschwind, L., Hartmann, F., van der Maarel, N., Papassotiropoulos, A., de Quervain, D., & Milnik, A. (2015). Sex-dependent dissociation between emotional appraisal and memory: A large-scale behavioral and fMRI study. *Journal of Neuroscience, 35*(3), 920–935. https://doi.org/10.1523/JNEUROSCI.2384-14.2015

Spear, L. P. (2000a). The adolescent brain and age-related behavioral manifestations. *Neuroscience & Behavioral Reviews, 24*(4), 417–463. https://doi.org/10.1016/S0149-7634(00)00014-2

Spear, L. P. (2000b). Neurobehavioral changes in adolescence. *Current Directions in Psychological Science, 9*(4), 111–114. https://doi.org/10.1111/1467-8721.00072

Spear, L. P. (2013). Adolescent neurodevelopment. *Journal of Adolescent Health, 52*(2), S7–S13. https://doi.org/10.1016/j.jadohealth.2012.05.006

Steinberg, L. (2001). We know some things: Parent-adolescent relationships in retrospect and prospect. *Journal of Research on Adolescence, 11*(1), 1–19. https://doi.org/10.1111/1532-7795.00001

Steinberg, L. (2011). *You and your adolescent: The essential guide for ages 10–25.* Simon & Schuster.

Stoet, G., O'Connor, D. B., Conner, M. T., & Laws, K. R. (2013). Are women better than men at multitasking? *BMS Psychology, 1,* Article 18. https://doi.org/10.1186/2050-7283-1-18

Stout, M. (2000). *The feel-good curriculum: The dumbing down of America's kids in the name of self-esteem.* De Capo Press.

Strauch, B. (2003). *The primal teen: What the new discoveries about the teenage brain tell us about our kids.* Doubleday.

Strean, W. B. (2009). Laughter prescription. *Canadian Family Physician, 55*(10), 965–967.

Strenziok, M., Krueger, F., Deshpande, G., Lenroot, R. K., van der Meer, E., & Grafman, J. (2010). Fronto-parietal regulation of media violence exposure in adolescents: A multi-method study. *Social, Cognitive and Affective Neuroscience, 6*(5), 537–547. https://doi.org/10.1093/scan/nsq079

Strenziok, M., Krueger, F., Pulaski, S. J., Openshaw, A. E., Zamboni, G., van der Meer, E., & Grafman, J. (2010). Lower lateral orbitofrontal cortex density associated with more frequent exposure to television and movie violence in male adolescents. *Journal of Adolescent Health, 46*(6), 607–609. https://doi.org/10.1016/j.jadohealth.2009.11.196

Sylwester, R. (1997). The neurobiology of self-esteem and aggression. *Educational Leadership, 54*(5), 75–79.

Sylwester, R. (2003). *A biological brain in a cultural classroom* (2nd ed.). Corwin Press.

Sylwester, R. (2005). *How to explain a brain: An educator's handbook of brain terms and cognitive processes.* Corwin Press.

Taylor, S. E., Klein, L. C., Lewis, B. P., Gruenewald, T. L., Gurung, R. A. R., & Updegraff, T. L. (2000). Biobehavioral responses to stress in females: Tend-and-befriend, not fight-or-flight. *Psychological Review, 107*(3), 411–429. https://doi.org/10.1037/0033-295X.107.3.411

Tenenbaum, H., Aznar, A., & Leman, P. (2014). Gender differences in language development. In P. J. Brooks & V. Kempe (Eds.), *Encyclopedia of language development* (pp. 229–232). SAGE Publications.

The Society for Neuroscience. (2002). *Brain facts: A primer on the brain and nervous system.* Everbest Printing Company.

Thompson, A. E., & Voyer, D. (2014). Sex differences in the ability to recognise non-verbal displays of emotion: A meta-analysis. *Cognition and Emotion, 28*(7), 1164–1165. https://doi.org/10.1080/02699931.2013.875889

Toga, A. W. & Thompson, P. M. (2003). Mapping brain asymmetry. *Nature Reviews Neuroscience, 4,* 37–48. https://doi.org/10.1038/nrn1009

Tokuhama-Espinosa, T. (2011). *Mind, brain and education science: A comprehensive guide to the new brain-based learning.* W. W. Norton & Company.

Torgrimson, B. N., & Minson, C. T. (2005). Sex and gender: What is the difference? *Journal of Applied Physiology, 99*(3), 785–787. https://doi.org/10.1152/japplphysiol.00376.2005

Twenge, J. M. (2017). *iGen: Why today's super-connected kids are growing up less rebellious, more tolerant, less happy and completely unprepared for adulthood.* Atria Books.

Twenge, J. M., Martin, G. N., & Campbell, W. K. (2018) Decreases in psychological well-being among American adolescents after 2012 and links to screen time during the rise of smartphone technology. *Emotion, 18*(6), 765–780. https://doi.org/10.1037/emo0000403

Urban, R. (2019, December 3). PISA global educational rankings: Schools fail on maths, science. *The Australian.*

Urgesi, C., Aglioti, S. M., Skrap, M., & Fabbro, F. (2010). The spiritual brain: Selective cortical lesions modulate human self-transcendence. *Neuron, 65*(3), 309–319. https://doi.org/10.1016/j.neuron.2010.01.026

Valeski, T. N., & Stipek, D. J. (2001). Young children's feelings about school. *Child Development, 72*(4), 1198–1213. https://doi.org/10.1111/1467-8624.00342

van Bokhoven, I., Van Goozen, S. H., van Engeland, H., Schaal, B., Arseneault, L., Seguin, J. R., Nagin, D. S., Vitaro, F., & Tremblay, R. E. (2005). Salivary cortisol and aggression in a population-based longitudinal study of adolescent males. *Journal of Neural Transmission, 112*(8), 1083–96. https://doi.org/10.1007/s00702-004-0253-5

Vanfossen, B., Brown, C. H., Kellam, S., Sokoloff, N., & Doering, S. (2010). Neighborhood context and the development of aggression in boys and girls. *Journal of Community Psychology, 38*(3), 329–349. https://doi.org/10.1002/jcop.20367

Verburgh, L., Königs, M., Scherder, E. J. A., & Oosterlaan, J. (2014). Physical exercise and executive functions in preadolescent children, adolescents and young adults: A meta-analysis. *British Journal of Sports Medicine, 48*(12), 973–979. http://dx.doi.org/10.1136/bjsports-2012-091441

Viner, R. M., Aswathikutty, G., Stiglic, N., Hudson, L. D., Goddings, A., Ward, J. L., & Nicholls, D. E. (2019). Roles of cyberbullying, sleep and physical activity in mediating the effects of social media use on mental health and wellbeing among young people in England: A secondary analysis of longitudinal data. *The Lancet: Child & Adolescent Health, 3*(10), 685–696. https://doi.org/10.1016/S2352-4642(19)30186-5

Wager, T. D., & Ochsner, K. N. (2005). Sex differences in the emotional brain. *NeuroReport, 16*(2), 85–87.

Walsh, F. (1998). *Strengthening family resilience.* The Guildford Press.

Wang, S. (2018). From birth onward, our experience of the world is dominated by the brain's continual conversation with itself. In D. J. Linden (Ed.), *Think tank: Forty neuroscientists explore the roots of human experience* (pp. 34–39). Yale University Press.

Wheelock, M. D., Hect, J. L., Hernandez-Andrade, E., Hassan, S. S., Romero, R., Eggebrecht, A. T., & Thomason, M. E. (2019). Sex differences in functional connectivity during fetal brain development. *Developmental Cognitive Neuroscience, 36,* 100632. https://doi.org/10.1016/j.dcn.2019.100632

Whitmire, R. (2012). *Why boys fail: Saving our sons from and educational system that's leaving them behind.* New York: American Management Association

Whittle, S., Yap, M. B. H., Yücel, M., Fornito, A., Simmons, J. G., Barrett, A., Sheeber, L., & Allen, N. B. (2008). Prefrontal and amygdala volumes are related to adolescents' affective behaviors during parent–adolescent interactions. *Proceedings of the National Academy of Sciences of the United States of America, 105*(9), 3652–3657. https://doi.org/10.1073/pnas.0709815105

Whittle, S., Yücel, M., Yap, M. B. H., & Allen, N. B. (2011). Sex differences in the neural correlates of emotion: Evidence from neuroimaging. *Biological Psychology, 87*(3), 319–333. https://doi.org/10.1016/j.biopsycho.2011.05.003

Wilson, T., & Shalley, F. (2018). Estimates of Australia's non-heterosexual population. *Australian Population Studies, 2*(1), 26–38. http://www.australianpopulationstudies.org/index.php/aps/article/view/23

Wingenbach, T. S. H., Ashwin, C., & Brosnan, M. (2018). Sex differences in facial emotion recognition across varying expression intensity levels from videos. *PLOS One, 13*(1), 1–18. https://doi.org/10.1371/journal.pone.0190634

Wolfe, P. (2001). *Brain matters: Translating research into classroom practice.* Association for Supervision and Curriculum Development.

Wright, A. (2000). *Spirituality and education.* RoutledgeFalmer.

Yarhouse, M. A. (2015). *Understanding gender dysphoria: Navigating transgender issues in a changing culture.* InterVarsity Press.

Yassin, A. A., Razak, N. A., & Maasum, N. (2018). Cooperative learning: General and theoretical background. *Advances in Social Sciences Research Journal, 5*(8), 642–654. https://doi.org/10.14738/assrj.58.5116

Yuan, J., Luo, Y., Yan, J. H., Meng, X., Yu, F., & Li, H. (2009). Neural correlates of the females' susceptibility to negative emotions: An insight into gender-related prevalence of affective disturbances, *Human Brain Mapping, 30*(11), 3676–3686. https://doi.org/10.1002/hbm.20796

Yue, Y., Shafto, P., Bonawitz, E., Yang, S. C. H., Golinkoff, R. M., Corriveau, K. H., Hirsch-Pasek, K., & Xu, F. (2018). The theoretical and methodological opportunities afforded by guided play with young children. *Frontiers in Psychology, 9,* Article 1152. https://doi.org/10.3389/fpsyg.2018.01152

Zak, P. J., & Barraza, J. A. (2013). The neurobiology of collective action. *Frontiers in Neuroscience, 7*(211), 1–9. https://doi.org/10.3389/fnins.2013.00211

Index

CPSIA information can be obtained
at www.ICGtesting.com
Printed in the USA
BVHW041028171021
619134BV00012B/881